Decoding the TOEFL® iBT

Actual Test

LISTENING 2

INTRODUCTION

For many learners of English, the TOEFL® iBT will be the most important standardized test they ever take. Unfortunately for a large number of these individuals, the material covered on the TOEFL® iBT remains a mystery to them, so they are unable to do well on the test. We hope that by using the *Decoding the TOEFL® iBT* series, individuals who take the TOEFL® iBT will be able to excel on the test and, in the process of using the book, may unravel the mysteries of the test and therefore make the material covered on the TOEFL® iBT more familiar to themselves.

The TOEFL® iBT covers the four main skills that a person must learn when studying any foreign language: reading, listening, speaking, and writing. The *Decoding the TOEFL® iBT* series contains books that cover all four of these skills. The *Decoding the TOEFL® iBT* series contains books with three separate levels for all four of the topics, and it also contains *Decoding the TOEFL® iBT Actual Test* books. These books contain several actual tests that learners can utilize to help them become better prepared to take the TOEFL® iBT. This book, *Decoding the TOEFL® iBT Actual Test Listening 2*, covers the listening aspect of the test and includes both conversations and lectures that are arranged in the same format as the TOEFL® iBT. Finally, the TOEFL® iBT underwent a number of changes in August 2019. This book—and the others in the series—takes those changes into account and incorporates them in the texts and questions, so readers of this second edition can be assured that they have up-to-date knowledge of the test.

Decoding the TOEFL® iBT Actual Test Listening 2 can be used by learners who are taking classes and also by individuals who are studying by themselves. It contains a total of eight full-length listening actual tests. Each actual test contains two conversations and three lectures. All of the conversations and lectures are the same length and have the same difficulty levels as those found on the TOEFL® iBT. In addition, the conversations and lectures contain the same numbers and types of questions that appear on the actual TOEFL® iBT, and the questions also have the same difficulty levels as those found on the TOEFL® iBT. Individuals who use *Decoding the TOEFL® iBT Actual Test Listening 2* will therefore be able to prepare themselves not only to take the TOEFL® iBT but also to perform well on the test.

We hope that everyone who uses *Decoding the TOEFL® iBT Actual Test Listening 2* will be able to become more familiar with the TOEFL® iBT and will additionally improve his or her score on the test. As the title of the book implies, we hope that learners can use it to crack the code on the TOEFL® iBT, to make the test itself less mysterious and confusing, and to get the highest score possible. Finally, we hope that both learners and instructors can use this book to its full potential. We wish all of you the best of luck as you study English and prepare for the TOEFL® iBT, and we hope that *Decoding the TOEFL® iBT Actual Test Listening 2* can provide you with assistance during the course of your studies.

Michael A. Putlack
Stephen Poirier
Maximilian Tolochko

TABLE
OF
CONTENTS

ABOUT THE TOEFL® iBT LISTENING SECTION

Changes in the Listening Section

TOEFL® underwent many changes in August of 2019. The following is an explanation of some of the changes that have been made to the Listening section.

Format

The Listening section contains either two or three parts. Before August 2019, each part had one conversation and two lectures. However, since the changes in August 2019, each part can have either one conversation and one lecture or one conversation and two lectures. In total, two conversations and three lectures (in two parts) or three conversations and four lectures (in three parts) can appear. The possible formats of the Listening section include the following:

Number of Parts	First Part	Second Part	Third Part
2	1 Conversation + 1 Lecture	1 Conversation + 2 Lectures	
	1 Conversation + 2 Lectures	1 Conversation + 1 Lecture	
3	1 Conversation + 1 Lecture	1 Conversation + 1 Lecture	1 Conversation + 2 Lectures
	1 Conversation + 1 Lecture	1 Conversation + 2 Lectures	1 Conversation + 1 Lecture
	1 Conversation + 2 Lectures	1 Conversation + 1 Lecture	1 Conversation + 1 Lecture

The time given for the Listening section has been reduced from 60-90 minutes to 41-57 minutes.

Passages and Questions

The lengths of the conversations and the lectures remain the same as before. The length of each conversation and lecture is 3 to 6 minutes.

It has been reported that some conversations have academic discussions that are of high difficulty levels, making them almost similar to lectures. For example, some questions might ask about academic information discussed between a student and a professor in the conversation. In addition, questions for both the conversations and the lectures tend to ask for more detailed information than before.

The numbers of questions remain the same. The test taker is given five questions after each conversation and six questions after each lecture. The time given for answering each set of questions is either 6.5 or 10 minutes.

Each conversation or lecture is heard only once. The test taker can take notes while listening to the passage and refer to them when answering the questions.

ABOUT THE TOEFL® iBT LISTENING SECTION

Question Types

TYPE 1 Gist-Content Questions

Gist-Content questions cover the test taker's basic comprehension of the listening passage. While they are typically asked after lectures, they are sometimes asked after conversations as well. These questions check to see if the test taker has understood the gist of the passage. They focus on the passage as a whole, so it is important to recognize what the main point of the lecture is or why the two people in the conversation are having a particular discussion. The test taker should therefore be able to recognize the theme of the lecture or conversation in order to answer this question correctly.

TYPE 2 Gist-Purpose Questions

Gist-Purpose questions cover the underlying theme of the passage. While they are typically asked after conversations, they are sometimes asked after lectures as well. Because these questions focus on the purpose or theme of the conversation or lecture, they begin with the word "why." They focus on the conversation or lecture as a whole, but they are not concerned with details; instead, they are concerned with why the student is speaking with the professor or employee or why the professor is covering a specific topic.

TYPE 3 Detail Questions

Detail questions cover the test taker's ability to understand facts and data that are mentioned in the listening passage. These questions appear after both conversations and lectures. Detail questions require the test taker to listen for and remember details from the passage. The majority of these questions concern major details that are related to the main topic of the lecture or conversation rather than minor ones. However, in some cases where there is a long digression that is not clearly related to the main idea, there may be a question about the details of the digression.

TYPE 4 Making Inferences Questions

Making Inferences questions cover the test taker's ability to understand implications made in the passage and to come to a conclusion about what these implications mean. These questions appear after both conversations and lectures. These questions require the test taker to hear the information being presented and then to make conclusions about what the information means or what is going to happen as a result of that information.

TYPE 5 Understanding Function Questions

Understanding Function questions cover the test taker's ability to determine the underlying meaning of what has been said in the passage. This question type often involves replaying a portion of the listening passage. There are two types of these questions. Some ask the test taker to infer the meaning of a phrase or a sentence. Thus the test taker needs to determine the implication—not the literal meaning— of the sentence. Other questions ask the test taker to infer the purpose of a statement made by one of the speakers. These questions specifically ask about the intended effect of a particular statement on the listener.

TYPE 6 Understanding Attitude Questions

Understanding Attitude questions cover the speaker's attitude or opinion toward something. These questions may appear after both lectures and conversations. This question type often involves replaying a portion of the listening passage. There are two types of these questions. Some ask about one of the speakers' feelings concerning something. These questions may check to see whether the test taker understands how a speaker feels about a particular topic, if a speaker likes or dislikes something, or why a speaker might feel anxiety or amusement. The other category asks about one of the speaker's opinions. These questions may inquire about a speaker's degree of certainty. Others may ask what a speaker thinks or implies about a topic, person, thing, or idea.

TYPE 7 Understanding Organization Questions

Understanding Organization questions cover the test taker's ability to determine the overall organization of the passage. These questions almost always appear after lectures. They rarely appear after conversations. These questions require the test taker to pay attention to two factors. The first is the way that the professor has organized the lecture and how he or she presents the information to the class. The second is how individual information given in the lecture relates to the lecture as a whole. To answer these questions correctly, test takers should focus more on the presentation and the professor's purpose in mentioning the facts rather than the facts themselves.

TYPE 8 Connecting Content Questions

Connecting Content questions almost exclusively appear after lectures, not after conversations. These questions measure the test taker's ability to understand how the ideas in the lecture relate to one another. These relationships may be explicitly stated, or you may have to infer them from the words you hear. The majority of these questions concern major relationships in the passage. These questions also commonly appear in passages where a number of different themes, ideas, objects, or individuals are being discussed.

Actual Test

\

01

Listening Section Directions

This section measures your ability to understand conversations and lectures in English.

The Listening section is divided into separately timed parts. In each part, you will listen to 1 conversation and 1 or 2 lectures. You will hear each conversation or lecture only one time.

After each conversation or lecture, you will answer some questions about it. The questions typically ask about the main idea and supporting details. Some questions ask about a speaker's purpose or attitude. Answer the questions based on what is stated or implied by the speakers.

You may take notes while you listen. You may use your notes to help you answer the questions. Your notes will not be scored.

If you need to change the volume while you listen, click on the **VOLUME ICON** at the top of the screen.

In some questions, you will see this icon: 🎧 This means that you will hear, but not see, part of the question.

Some of the questions have special directions. These directions appear in a gray box on the screen.

Most questions are worth 1 point. If a question is worth more than 1 point, it will have special directions that indicate how many points you can receive.

A clock at the top of the screen will show you how much time is remaining. The clock will not count down while you are listening. The clock will count down only while you are answering the questions.

🎧 AT01-01

1 Why did the professor ask to see the student?

    Ⓐ To remind her to submit a homework assignment next week

    Ⓑ To inform her about an upcoming contest she should enter

    Ⓒ To discuss a painting that she recently made in his class

    Ⓓ To talk about a report that the student needs to turn in soon

2 What can be inferred about the student?

    Ⓐ She is currently enrolled at the school as a junior.

    Ⓑ She is double-majoring in Art History and Fine Arts.

    Ⓒ She will take a class with the professor next semester.

    Ⓓ She is considering transferring to another school.

3 What will the student probably do next?

    Ⓐ Leave the office and go to her next class

    Ⓑ Show the professor a picture that she painted

    Ⓒ Look at a brochure together with the professor

    Ⓓ Discuss which classes she will take next semester

4   Listen again to part of the conversation. Then answer the question.

What does the professor mean when he says this:

  Ⓐ The student has a great deal of skill as an artist.

  Ⓑ The student should be able to sell some of her paintings.

  Ⓒ The student ought to try to improve her artistic abilities.

  Ⓓ The student needs to consider a future career in art.

5   Listen again to part of the conversation. Then answer the question.

What does the professor imply when he says this:

  Ⓐ The student should have no problem paying her tuition next year.

  Ⓑ There is a strong chance the student will win the contest.

  Ⓒ He believes the student is more likely to come in second or third.

  Ⓓ The prizes for second place and third place are cash awards.

AT01-02

Art History

etching

Daniel Hopfer

Rembrandt

6   What is the main topic of the lecture?

 Ⓐ The process through which etching was invented

 Ⓑ The most famous etchers of the 1600s

 Ⓒ The possibility that etching was invented in ancient times

 Ⓓ The early history of etching and how it is done

7   Why does the professor mention Daniel Hopfer?

 Ⓐ To talk about the historical importance of his work in etching

 Ⓑ To credit him with discovering that acid bites into copper better than iron

 Ⓒ To discuss the quality of the iron plates that he made as an armorer

 Ⓓ To state that he was from Northern Italy rather than Germany

8   In the lecture, the professor explains the process in which an etching is made. Put the steps in the correct order.

Drag each sentence to the space where it belongs.

1	
2	
3	
4	

 Ⓐ Ink is put onto a metal plate.

 Ⓑ Designs are cut into the wax by an artist.

 Ⓒ A metal plate is covered in wax.

 Ⓓ A metal plate is dipped into some acid.

9   What is the professor's opinion of Rembrandt's etchings?

Ⓐ Their quality is extremely high.

Ⓑ They are limited in their subject matter.

Ⓒ They are primitive in appearance.

Ⓓ They look better than those of any other etcher.

10 What does the professor imply about Rembrandt?

Ⓐ He preferred to make etchings instead of paintings.

Ⓑ He learned to make etchings from Daniel Hopfer.

Ⓒ He became wealthy by selling so many etchings.

Ⓓ He made multiple bitings of many of his etchings.

11 What will the professor probably do next?

Ⓐ Have the students make their own etchings

Ⓑ Show some pictures to the class

Ⓒ Tell the students about their midterm exam

Ⓓ Ask the students some questions

PART 2 Conversation

AT01-03

1 What problem does the student have?

(A) He has a time conflict with an upcoming sporting event.

(B) He needs to study on the weekend instead of playing sports.

(C) He suffered an injury and may not be able to play in a tournament.

(D) He has no way to get to his interview on Saturday.

2 In the conversation, the student describes a number of facts about his interview. Indicate whether each of the following is a fact or not.

Click in the correct box for each statement.

	Fact	Not a Fact
1 It is for a position that is related to his major.		
2 It will be conducted by five different people.		
3 It is going to begin at eleven in the morning.		
4 It will take place at the company's office in Anniston.		

3 Why does the coach tell the student about Coach Patterson?

(A) To point out that he frequently helps other team members

(B) To ask the student if he knows who Coach Patterson is

(C) To explain how he intends to deal with the student's problem

(D) To make a joke about what Coach Patterson's role is

4 What can be inferred about the student?

     Ⓐ He is recovering from a recent injury.

     Ⓑ He has been on the team for three years.

     Ⓒ He is a starter on the basketball team.

     Ⓓ He plays on the soccer team with Clark and Don.

5 Listen again to part of the conversation. Then answer the question.

What is the purpose of the student's response?

     Ⓐ To point out his lack of a driver's license

     Ⓑ To agree with the coach's opinion

     Ⓒ To reject the coach's suggestion

     Ⓓ To indicate his willingness to buy a car

AT01-04

Psychology

6 What is the main topic of the lecture?

  (A) Various types of memories that people acquire

  (B) The need to have an emotional response to remember something

  (C) Collective memory and what kinds of events can trigger it

  (D) The factors involved in which events people remember

7 What is the likely outcome of a person who is involved in a traumatic accident as a child?

  (A) The person will remember the event for a long time.

  (B) The person will be afraid of that animal for the rest of his or her life.

  (C) The person will forget about the event fairly quickly.

  (D) The person will develop a collective memory of the event.

8 According to the professor, what can happen when people keep certain memories secret?

  (A) They may come to believe that the events in their memories never took place.

  (B) They may recall the events in those memories for the rest of their lives.

  (C) They may start to think that the memories belong to someone else rather than themselves.

  (D) They may develop illusive memories and fail to recall the events accurately.

9 Why does the professor tell the students about the car accident she witnessed?

    Ⓐ To prove that she has an excellent memory

    Ⓑ To show the students what an illusive memory is

    Ⓒ To provide an example of a collective memory

    Ⓓ To encourage the students to discuss similar events in their lives

10 What event does the professor say can cause people to get tunnel memory?

    Ⓐ An assassination

    Ⓑ A bank robbery

    Ⓒ An explosion

    Ⓓ An animal attack

11 Listen again to part of the lecture. Then answer the question.

What does the professor imply when she says this:

    Ⓐ The student gave the answer that she had expected him to.

    Ⓑ She believes that the student actually can remember what happened.

    Ⓒ The student needs to focus his mind to recall the event.

    Ⓓ She wants the class to think about the question she just asked.

AT01-05

Physics

magnetism

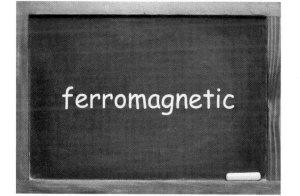

ferromagnetic

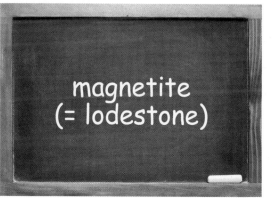

magnetite
(= lodestone)

12 What can be inferred about the professor?

    Ⓐ He intends to give the students a quiz at the end of the class.

    Ⓑ He conducts research on magnetism and its effects on materials.

    Ⓒ He hopes that the students will offer their opinions on the subject.

    Ⓓ He will discuss topics other than magnetism in today's class.

13 What comparison does the professor make between copper and magnetite?

    Ⓐ The strengths of their magnetic fields

    Ⓑ The number of electrons in their electron clouds

    Ⓒ The ways people make use of them

    Ⓓ The names that they were called in the past

14 What is the professor's opinion of temporary magnets?

    Ⓐ They have some uses.

    Ⓑ They are worthless.

    Ⓒ They are not powerful enough.

    Ⓓ They are hard to create.

15 According to the professor, what helps create a magnetic field in an atom?

    Ⓐ The number of electrons that it has

    Ⓑ The way its protons and neutrons interact

    Ⓒ The size and shape of its nucleus

    Ⓓ The direction that its electrons spin

16 Why does the professor discuss helium's lack of a magnetic field?

    Ⓐ To compare it with iron and copper

    Ⓑ To point out that it only has two electrons

    Ⓒ To provide an example for the students

    Ⓓ To mention that it has very few uses

17 What will the professor probably do next?

    Ⓐ Begin to discuss a new topic

    Ⓑ Show some slides to the students

    Ⓒ Speak about electromagnets

    Ⓓ Give the students a handout

Actual Test

02

Listening Section Directions

This section measures your ability to understand conversations and lectures in English.

The Listening section is divided into separately timed parts. In each part, you will listen to 1 conversation and 1 or 2 lectures. You will hear each conversation or lecture only one time.

After each conversation or lecture, you will answer some questions about it. The questions typically ask about the main idea and supporting details. Some questions ask about a speaker's purpose or attitude. Answer the questions based on what is stated or implied by the speakers.

You may take notes while you listen. You may use your notes to help you answer the questions. Your notes will not be scored.

If you need to change the volume while you listen, click on the **VOLUME ICON** at the top of the screen.

In some questions, you will see this icon: 🎧 This means that you will hear, but not see, part of the question.

Some of the questions have special directions. These directions appear in a gray box on the screen.

Most questions are worth 1 point. If a question is worth more than 1 point, it will have special directions that indicate how many points you can receive.

A clock at the top of the screen will show you how much time is remaining. The clock will not count down while you are listening. The clock will count down only while you are answering the questions.

PART 1 Conversation

🎧 AT02-01

1   Why does the student visit the student housing office?

   Ⓐ The man called her and requested that she visit.

   Ⓑ The student received an email requesting her presence.

   Ⓒ Her resident assistant ordered her to go to the office.

   Ⓓ She received a note telling her she needed to go there.

2   What is the student's attitude toward the man?

   Ⓐ She is unwilling to give him any information.

   Ⓑ She is impatient and displeased with him.

   Ⓒ She is upset that he is making her miss her class.

   Ⓓ She is surprised that he wants to speak to her.

3   What did the student remove from her room?

   Ⓐ Curtains

   Ⓑ The bed

   Ⓒ Blinds

   Ⓓ The desk

4   Why does the student have to pay the student housing office?

    Click on 2 answers.

    1.   She caused some damage to her dormitory room.

    2.   She must pay a fine for improperly removing furniture.

    3.   She was too noisy and disturbed some of the other students.

    4.   She needs to pay a storage fee for the item she removed.

5   What can be inferred about the student?

    A.   She is shocked that she has to pay so much money.

    B.   She is going to move to off-campus housing soon.

    C.   She intends to protest the amount of money she must pay.

    D.   She plans to move to a room in a different dormitory.

AT02-02

Economics

6   What is the lecture mainly about?

  Ⓐ The reason that Spain's nobility attained so much power

  Ⓑ The effects that the American colonies of Spain had on it

  Ⓒ The manner in which Spain acquired its overseas empire

  Ⓓ The different classes of people in Spain during the 1500s

7   Why does the professor discuss the attitude of the Spanish nobility in the 1500s?

  Ⓐ To point out why Spain was involved in so many wars during that time

  Ⓑ To blame their manner of thought on the Spanish Inquisition

  Ⓒ To accuse them of thinking poorly of the peasantry and merchant class

  Ⓓ To mention why so few of them ever became members of the clergy

8   According to the professor, what negative effects did Spain suffer in the 1500s?

  Click on 2 answers.

  1 It became difficult for people to find even the most basic goods.

  2 Many of Spain's most talented people departed to live in its colonies.

  3 Crop failures and plagues resulted in a dramatic population decline.

  4 The country lost almost all of the wars that it fought against other nations.

9 What does the professor imply about Spain in the 1500s?

    Ⓐ It is highly surprising that the peasants did not revolt against the nobles there.

    Ⓑ It would have been better off had it not founded any American colonies.

    Ⓒ It went from being the most powerful European country to the weakest one.

    Ⓓ It lost a greater percentage of its population than both England and France did.

10 Listen again to part of the lecture. Then answer the question.

Why does the professor say this:

    Ⓐ To declare that Spain's wealth should have provided more advantages to the country

    Ⓑ To confess that he believes Spain should have attempted to acquire more wealth

    Ⓒ To admit that he does not understand why Spain suffered so much during that time

    Ⓓ To note that Spain's money caused it problems rather than solving them

11 Listen again to part of the lecture. Then answer the question.

What does the professor imply when he says this:

    Ⓐ The ships in the convoys were often attacked while at sea.

    Ⓑ Many of the pirates were sponsored by Spain's enemies.

    Ⓒ Almost all of the ships in the convoys were sunk at times.

    Ⓓ Spain became much wealthier than all of its enemies.

AT02-03

Environmental Science

Franz Joseph Land

©Oona Raisanen

keystone species

a little auk

12 Why does the professor explain what a keystone species is?

    (A) She considers the definition in the textbook to be inadequate.

    (B) She wants to correct a student who gives an improper explanation of it.

    (C) She is responding to a request by a student for her to define it.

    (D) She is contrasting its meaning with that of another similar term.

13 According to the professor, what is the main problem in Franz Joseph Land?

    (A) The icecaps located in the region are decreasing in size.

    (B) Too many animals are living in a relatively small location.

    (C) There is not enough biodiversity in the entire region.

    (D) The keystone species in the area is going extinct.

14 What is the likely outcome of the ice in Franz Joseph Land expanding?

Click on 2 answers.

    1 Polar bears will have a harder time finding prey due to all of the ice.

    2 The copepods living in the nearby waters will become more numerous.

    3 A large number of animals will see their main food supply increase.

    4 There will be more places for birds such as the little auk to nest.

15 What does the professor imply about the polar bears residing in Franz Joseph Land?

  Ⓐ They are catching fewer seals and walruses these days.

  Ⓑ They have begun hunting smaller prey such as the little auk.

  Ⓒ They have seen their numbers decrease by half recently.

  Ⓓ They weigh less than polar bears living in other parts of the Arctic.

16 How is the lecture organized?

  Ⓐ The professor focuses on explaining how a serious problem can be solved.

  Ⓑ The professor describes the cause of a problem and its effects on humans.

  Ⓒ The professor mentions a problem and then describes some possible results.

  Ⓓ The professor explains a current situation and the reasons that it happened.

17 Listen again to part of the lecture. Then answer the question.

  What does the professor imply when she says this:

  Ⓐ She wants the students to understand precisely how the islands were formed.

  Ⓑ There are no other islands in the world similar to those in Franz Joseph Land.

  Ⓒ She can give more details to the students who are interested in geology.

  Ⓓ The information she is providing is not relevant to the rest of her lecture.

1 Why does the student visit the professor?

    Ⓐ To ask about a homework assignment she submitted

    Ⓑ To find out when she normally has her office hours

    Ⓒ To learn how she can make her paper better

    Ⓓ To inquire about a grade she received on a recent exam

2 Why does the professor apologize to the student?

    Ⓐ She made a mistake while grading the student's midterm exam.

    Ⓑ She is unaware of what the student's name is.

    Ⓒ She forgot to give the student a handout that she needs.

    Ⓓ She only has a limited amount of time to speak with the student.

3 What is the student's opinion of the score she got on her test?

    Ⓐ It is much higher than she had expected to receive.

    Ⓑ It is much lower than she had expected to receive.

    Ⓒ It is right about what she had expected to receive.

    Ⓓ It is a few points higher than she had expected to receive.

4 What advice does the professor give the student?

Click on 2 answers.

1. Read all of the material that is assigned on the syllabus
2. Take notes while the professor is lecturing to the class
3. Sit closer to the front of the class rather than in the back
4. Stop being ten or fifteen minutes late for class each time

5 Listen again to part of the conversation. Then answer the question.

What can be inferred about the student when she says this:

- (A) She expects the professor to be in her office for a while.
- (B) She has to attend another class later in the afternoon.
- (C) She is embarrassed that she cannot find her test paper.
- (D) She lives in a dormitory located across from the professor's building.

AT02-05

Anthropology

the Bering Strait

Old Crow Basin

the Clovis site

Monte Verde

6 What is the lecture mainly about?

 Ⓐ The manner in which North and South America were populated

 Ⓑ The dig sites that have been found in Clovis and Monte Verde

 Ⓒ The accuracy of the theory on how people first arrived in the Americas

 Ⓓ The most likely explanation for how people first came to the Americas

7 Why does the professor discuss the formation of a land bridge across the Bering Strait?

 Ⓐ To point out how ancient people were believed to have arrived in the Americas

 Ⓑ To claim that it does not appear every time there is an ice age on the planet

 Ⓒ To express his skepticism that people were actually able to walk across it

 Ⓓ To state that not only people but also animals crossed into the Americas on it

8 What was found at Old Crow Basin?

 Ⓐ Spear points

 Ⓑ Chipped bones

 Ⓒ An ancient settlement

 Ⓓ Human remains

9   What is the professor's opinion of the Monte Verde settlers?

    Ⓐ They were the first people proven to be in the Americas.

    Ⓑ They did not arrive as early as some people think.

    Ⓒ They arrived in the Americas by sailing on boats.

    Ⓓ They made use of tools that were advanced for their time.

10   How is the lecture organized?

    Ⓐ The professor covers the events in chronological order.

    Ⓑ The professor asks questions and encourages the students to answer them.

    Ⓒ The professor discusses various sites and what was found in them.

    Ⓓ The professor mentions certain theories in order of their likelihood.

11   Listen again to part of the lecture. Then answer the question.

    What can be inferred about the professor when he says this:

    Ⓐ He fully agrees with the student's comments.

    Ⓑ He thinks the student omitted some crucial information.

    Ⓒ He intends to discuss the matter in more detail.

    Ⓓ He considers the student an expert on the topic.

Actual Test

03

Listening Section Directions

This section measures your ability to understand conversations and lectures in English.

The Listening section is divided into separately timed parts. In each part, you will listen to 1 conversation and 1 or 2 lectures. You will hear each conversation or lecture only one time.

After each conversation or lecture, you will answer some questions about it. The questions typically ask about the main idea and supporting details. Some questions ask about a speaker's purpose or attitude. Answer the questions based on what is stated or implied by the speakers.

You may take notes while you listen. You may use your notes to help you answer the questions. Your notes will not be scored.

If you need to change the volume while you listen, click on the **VOLUME ICON** at the top of the screen.

In some questions, you will see this icon: 🎧 This means that you will hear, but not see, part of the question.

Some of the questions have special directions. These directions appear in a gray box on the screen.

Most questions are worth 1 point. If a question is worth more than 1 point, it will have special directions that indicate how many points you can receive.

A clock at the top of the screen will show you how much time is remaining. The clock will not count down while you are listening. The clock will count down only while you are answering the questions.

AT03-01

1 What are the speakers mainly discussing?

    (A) Taking notes the proper way in class

    (B) The student's upcoming final exam

    (C) The injury that the student suffered

    (D) Makeup work that the student must do

2 According to the professor, how did she learn about the student's injury?

    (A) The student's parents called her to talk about it.

    (B) She was informed about it by the dean of students.

    (C) There was an article about it in the school newspaper.

    (D) The student's academic advisor spoke to her about it.

3 In the conversation, the student and professor describe a number of facts about the midterm exam. Indicate whether each of the following is a fact or not.

Click in the correct box for each statement.

	Fact	Not a Fact
1 The other students took the exam two weeks ago.		
2 The student will take the exam in one week.		
3 The exam for the student will be held in the professor's office.		
4 The materials covered while the student missed class will be on the exam.		

4　What will the professor probably do next?

   Ⓐ Read the note from the student's doctor that he gave her

   Ⓑ Speak to the student about the paper that he wrote

   Ⓒ Let the student copy some of her notes for the class

   Ⓓ Look for a handout that she needs to give to the student

5　Listen again to part of the conversation. Then answer the question.

What can be inferred from the professor's response to the student?

   Ⓐ She believes that Emily Jackson takes excellent notes in her class.

   Ⓑ She would like the student to speak with his friend about the matter.

   Ⓒ Emily Jackson received the highest grade on the test in her class.

   Ⓓ Students in her class are responsible for taking notes during her lectures.

AT03-02

Geology

gorges

the Grand Canyon

the Vikos Gorge

6   What is the main topic of the lecture?

    Ⓐ The deepest gorges in the world

    Ⓑ The ways that gorges can be created

    Ⓒ The gorges in the United States

    Ⓓ The similarities between canyons and gorges

7   Why does the professor mention limestone?

    Ⓐ To point out its role in forming gorges with steep sides

    Ⓑ To claim that it takes a long time for gorges to form in it

    Ⓒ To note how strong it is in comparison to other rocks

    Ⓓ To state that geological uplift can create gorges in it

8   According to the professor, what is a common feature of gorges formed by geological uplift?

    Ⓐ They rarely have rivers or streams at their bottoms.

    Ⓑ They can extend for hundreds of kilometers.

    Ⓒ They have waterfalls in certain areas.

    Ⓓ They are deeper than other types of gorges.

9 Based on the information in the lecture, indicate which geological process that causes gorges to form the statements refer to.

Click in the correct box for each statement.

	Erosion	Glacial Action
1 Is the method that created the Columbia River Gorge		
2 Can be created through the action of flowing water		
3 Usually has its bottom at the same level as the body of water its river empties into		
4 Often creates a river at the same time a gorge is formed		

10 Why does the professor tell the students to look at the screen?

Ⓐ To have them see an image of the Grand Canyon

Ⓑ To present a chart on the world's deepest gorges

Ⓒ To show them a short video of the Vikos Gorge

Ⓓ To provide a graph on how geological uplift works

11 How does the professor organize the information about gorges that he presents to the class?

Ⓐ By talking about some famous gorges and explaining how they were made

Ⓑ By showing pictures of some gorges and then mentioning ways to tell how they were created

Ⓒ By describing in detail each of the three ways that gorges can be created over time

Ⓓ By discussing the most common manner that gorges are made in great detail

AT03-03

1 Why did the guidance counselor ask to see the student?

   Ⓐ She schedules meetings with every student at least once a year.

   Ⓑ His parents called her and requested that she have a talk with him.

   Ⓒ She received a report from the dean that his grades are poor.

   Ⓓ Some professors expressed their concern about the student to her.

2 What advice does the guidance counselor give the student?

   Ⓐ To attend extra study sessions for his classes

   Ⓑ To engage in some leisurely activities at times

   Ⓒ To request extensions on his work from his professors

   Ⓓ To spend as much time as possible at the library

3 What will the student probably do next?

   Ⓐ Go to a meeting he has scheduled with his advisor

   Ⓑ Continue to speak with the guidance counselor

   Ⓒ Attend his last class of the day

   Ⓓ Schedule another appointment with the guidance counselor

4   Listen again to part of the conversation. Then answer the question.

What does the guidance counselor mean when she says this:

   Ⓐ The student should trust everything that she says to him.

   Ⓑ The information that the student requested cannot be given to him.

   Ⓒ She has a strict policy on what she can speak about with students.

   Ⓓ She will not talk about their conversation with anyone else.

5   Listen again to part of the conversation. Then answer the question.

What does the student imply when he says this:

   Ⓐ Studying a great deal is unlikely to help him do well in his classes.

   Ⓑ He is going to get the lowest grades of his college life this semester.

   Ⓒ It is likely that he is going to drop out of school soon.

   Ⓓ He cannot handle the class load that he is taking this term.

AT03-04

History

6 What aspect of the Byzantine Empire does the professor mainly discuss?

Ⓐ Its battles against Islam

Ⓑ Its relationship with the West

Ⓒ Its legacy

Ⓓ Its intellectual knowledge

7 Why does the professor mention the Battle of Tours?

Ⓐ To emphasize its historical importance

Ⓑ To describe the Byzantine role at it

Ⓒ To focus on the tactics that helped win it

Ⓓ To explain where the battle was fought

8 How did the Byzantine Empire help Western Europe?

Click on 2 answers.

1 It defeated barbarians attacking the Western Roman Empire.

2 It protected the Europeans from invaders from the east.

3 It provided information that helped lead to the Renaissance.

4 It sent armies to fight against Muslim invaders in the west.

9 According to the professor, what was a result of the Muslim conquest of Constantinople?

 Ⓐ The Crusaders assembled to try to take back the Holy Land.

 Ⓑ Most of the land routes to Asian became much safer.

 Ⓒ There was renewed interest in learning about ancient Greece and Rome.

 Ⓓ Western Europeans began looking for new trade routes.

10 What will the professor probably do next?

 Ⓐ Discuss the final exam with the class

 Ⓑ Continue to lecture to the students

 Ⓒ Hand the students back their papers

 Ⓓ Answer a question from a student

11 Listen again to part of the lecture. Then answer the question.

 What can be inferred about the professor when he says this:

 Ⓐ He is considered a leading scholar on the Renaissance.

 Ⓑ He thinks the Renaissance was the Byzantine Empire's greatest contribution to history.

 Ⓒ He believes Renaissance history is more interesting than Byzantine history.

 Ⓓ He is going to teach a class on the Renaissance in the next semester.

AT03-05

Zoology

badgers

sett

12 According to the professor, what does a badger look like?

    (A) It is around one meter long and has stripes on its entire body.

    (B) It is a short animal with a long neck and gray fur on its body.

    (C) It is a fierce-looking animal with long, sharp teeth and claws.

    (D) It has long legs and long claws but a fairly short body.

13 What can be inferred about the badger?

    (A) It is willing to attack animals more dangerous than it.

    (B) It can survive well in all kinds of environments.

    (C) It is currently an endangered species due to hunters.

    (D) It is immune to the venom of some species of snakes.

14 In the lecture, the professor describes a number of facts about the badger's sett. Indicate whether each of the following is a fact or not.

Click in the correct box for each statement.

	Fact	Not a Fact
1 The badger has a special room in the sett that it uses for a latrine.		
2 It can have more than ten entrances.		
3 It contains no garbage or food.		
4 Up to twenty badgers may live in a single sett.		

15 How is the lecture organized?

    Ⓐ The professor describes the traits of several different species of badgers.

    Ⓑ The professor compares and contrasts two different species of badgers.

    Ⓒ The professor focuses primarily on describing the features of the honey badger.

    Ⓓ The professor provides a number of facts about the characteristics of badgers.

16 What will the professor probably do next?

    Ⓐ Give the students an assignment

    Ⓑ Describe one more characteristic of badgers

    Ⓒ Let the students leave the classroom

    Ⓓ Start talking about the American badger

17 Listen again to part of the lecture. Then answer the question.

What does the professor mean when he says this:

    Ⓐ There are some foods badgers cannot eat.

    Ⓑ Badgers will eat virtually anything.

    Ⓒ Badgers eat both plants and animals.

    Ⓓ Most badgers prefer to consume meat.

Actual Test

04

Listening Section Directions

This section measures your ability to understand conversations and lectures in English.

The Listening section is divided into separately timed parts. In each part, you will listen to 1 conversation and 1 or 2 lectures. You will hear each conversation or lecture only one time.

After each conversation or lecture, you will answer some questions about it. The questions typically ask about the main idea and supporting details. Some questions ask about a speaker's purpose or attitude. Answer the questions based on what is stated or implied by the speakers.

You may take notes while you listen. You may use your notes to help you answer the questions. Your notes will not be scored.

If you need to change the volume while you listen, click on the **VOLUME ICON** at the top of the screen.

In some questions, you will see this icon: 🎧 This means that you will hear, but not see, part of the question.

Some of the questions have special directions. These directions appear in a gray box on the screen.

Most questions are worth 1 point. If a question is worth more than 1 point, it will have special directions that indicate how many points you can receive.

A clock at the top of the screen will show you how much time is remaining. The clock will not count down while you are listening. The clock will count down only while you are answering the questions.

AT04-01

1   Why does the student tell the secretary about Professor Wright?

   Ⓐ To note that she just had a meeting in his office

   Ⓑ To explain how she learned about the position

   Ⓒ To determine if he needs a student assistant

   Ⓓ To mention that he is her academic advisor

2   What is the student's attitude toward the duties of the job?

   Ⓐ She feels that the duties will be too time consuming.

   Ⓑ She expresses a desire to learn how to do each of them.

   Ⓒ She believes most of the work will be very boring.

   Ⓓ She is fine doing the work that the secretary mentions.

3   According to the secretary, what is a student who does the job required to do?

   Click on 2 answers.

   ① Do office work such as filing

   ② Assist professors with their lectures

   ③ Do research for some graduate students

   ④ Run errands to different departments

4 Which type of work schedule does the secretary say is the best?

    Ⓐ Three hours a day three days a week

    Ⓑ Three hours a day four days a week

    Ⓒ Four hours a day two days a week

    Ⓓ Four hours a day three days a week

5 What can be inferred about the student?

    Ⓐ She intends to accept the job if it is offered to her.

    Ⓑ She wants to earn money in order to pay her tuition.

    Ⓒ She has a double major in History and English.

    Ⓓ She hopes to work in the office during summer vacation.

AT04-02

Astronomy

6 What is the main topic of the lecture?

Ⓐ How extraterrestrial life will most likely appear

Ⓑ The chances that alien life exists in the universe

Ⓒ The requirements for life existing on a planet or moon

Ⓓ How astronomers are searching for alien life

7 What is the professor's opinion on the existence of alien life?

Ⓐ It definitely exists elsewhere in the universe.

Ⓑ It has already been proven to exist in other places.

Ⓒ Earth is the only place in the universe with life on it.

Ⓓ There is a tiny chance that life exists elsewhere.

8 What does the professor imply about alien life?

Ⓐ It will almost surely resemble humans in appearance.

Ⓑ It will most likely be hostile to life on the Earth.

Ⓒ It may be much more intelligent than humans.

Ⓓ It may be able to breathe gases other than oxygen.

9   According to the professor, what will the majority of alien life be like?

   Ⓐ Very tiny creatures

   Ⓑ Fishlike creatures

   Ⓒ Bipeds that look like humans

   Ⓓ Creatures with mechanical implements

10   Why does the professor tell the students about high-gravity environments?

   Ⓐ To point out that life on them will not be bipedal

   Ⓑ To stress that they are unlikely to have any life on them

   Ⓒ To claim that they are strong candidates for alien life

   Ⓓ To mention how frequently they appear in the galaxy

11   What can be inferred about aliens that may live on gas giants?

   Ⓐ They will have a large number of legs to enable easy movement.

   Ⓑ They will probably rely upon oxygen in order to breathe.

   Ⓒ They will look different from those that live on watery worlds.

   Ⓓ They will be large in size but likely low in intelligence

AT04-03

History

hedges

the enclosure movement

12 What aspect of hedges does the professor mainly discuss?

  Ⓐ Their role in the history of land usage in England

  Ⓑ The contributions they made to the Industrial Revolution

  Ⓒ How landowners used them to enclose their property

  Ⓓ What kinds of plants were used to create them

13 When did people in England first start planting hedges?

  Ⓐ When the Middle Ages began

  Ⓑ When the Romans lived in England

  Ⓒ When the Anglo-Saxon Period happened

  Ⓓ When the Industrial Revolution started

14 What does the professor imply about the open field system?

  Ⓐ It was created on account of a law passed by Parliament.

  Ⓑ The English used it both in England and in their overseas colonies.

  Ⓒ The common people used it to cut down trees to build their homes with.

  Ⓓ It was disliked by people who owned large amounts of property.

15 Why does the professor discuss the Industrial Revolution?

Ⓐ To point out that it started in England and spread elsewhere

Ⓑ To respond to the student's request to talk about it

Ⓒ To mention several ways that it improved England's economy

Ⓓ To explain why so many hedges were planted during it

16 What is the professor's attitude toward the student?

Ⓐ She is impressed by his thought process.

Ⓑ She thinks he overlooks an important point.

Ⓒ She is discouraged by his answer to her question.

Ⓓ She respects him for admitting he cannot answer her question.

17 According to the professor, what happened in England as a result of the enclosure movement?

Click on 2 answers.

☐ Parliament made laws defending the landowners' actions.

☐ Less land was farmed, so many common people starved.

☐ Many people living in the countryside moved to the cities.

☐ English farmers raised more sheep than people in any other country.

AT04-04

1   What are the speakers mainly discussing?

    Ⓐ The topic of the student's senior thesis

    Ⓑ The type of research that the student will have to do

    Ⓒ The student's desire to write a senior thesis next year

    Ⓓ The best way to determine what the student should write about

2   According to the student, what does he plan to do next year?

Click on 2 answers.

    1 Find an internship at a company

    2 Study abroad during the fall semester

    3 Quit playing for a sports team

    4 Work part time in the library

3   Why does the professor ask the student about his plans for next year?

    Ⓐ To determine whether his workload is going to be too heavy

    Ⓑ To find out which semester he wants to write his thesis during

    Ⓒ To ask if he intends to do any of his research while he is abroad

    Ⓓ To learn when he is going to find the time to do his research

4   What is the professor going to give the student tomorrow?

    Ⓐ A senior thesis written by a previous student

    Ⓑ A list of books that he needs to look at

    Ⓒ Some topics he should consider writing about

    Ⓓ Information on the academic requirements for writing a thesis

5   What can be inferred about the professor?

    Ⓐ She is going to let the student read her own thesis.

    Ⓑ She has agreed to serve as the student's thesis advisor.

    Ⓒ She has never assisted a student in writing a thesis.

    Ⓓ She believes the student is unqualified to write a thesis.

AT04-05

Environmental
Science

6 What aspect of lakes in winter does the professor mainly discuss?

Click on 2 answers.

1. How some fish react when the water gets cooler
2. The manner that oxygen gets added to the water
3. The process through which lakes partially freeze
4. The way that fish can reproduce during that time

7 According to the professor, when does the water in a cooling lake stop cycling up and down?

(A) When the temperature of the air goes below four degrees Celsius

(B) When the upper layer of the lake declines to zero degrees Celsius

(C) When the entire lake's temperature reaches four degrees Celsius

(D) When the temperature of the air gets down to zero degrees Celsius

8 What is a result of fish slowing down their metabolisms in winter?

(A) They can avoid eating for up to a month.

(B) They have no need to hide from other fish.

(C) They do not feel an urge to reproduce.

(D) They require less oxygen to breathe.

9   Why does the professor discuss the trout?

    Ⓐ To note the types of food it eats when lakes begin to freeze

    Ⓑ To describe some ways in which its activity increases in winter

    Ⓒ To state that it moves into areas occupied by northern pike and carp

    Ⓓ To claim that it hunts fish that can no longer hide in plants

10   What comparison does the professor make between walleye and bass?

    Ⓐ Which foods they consume

    Ⓑ How active they are in winter

    Ⓒ Which lakes they can be found in

    Ⓓ How they slow down their metabolisms

11   Listen again to part of the lecture. Then answer the question.

    What does the professor imply when he says this:

    Ⓐ The digestive systems of various species of fish differ greatly.

    Ⓑ A large number of fish do not survive the winter months.

    Ⓒ Fish can eat much less than normal during winter.

    Ⓓ Only a few fish can slow down their metabolisms in winter.

Actual Test

05

Listening Section Directions

This section measures your ability to understand conversations and lectures in English.

The Listening section is divided into separately timed parts. In each part, you will listen to 1 conversation and 1 or 2 lectures. You will hear each conversation or lecture only one time.

After each conversation or lecture, you will answer some questions about it. The questions typically ask about the main idea and supporting details. Some questions ask about a speaker's purpose or attitude. Answer the questions based on what is stated or implied by the speakers.

You may take notes while you listen. You may use your notes to help you answer the questions. Your notes will not be scored.

If you need to change the volume while you listen, click on the **VOLUME ICON** at the top of the screen.

In some questions, you will see this icon: 🎧 This means that you will hear, but not see, part of the question.

Some of the questions have special directions. These directions appear in a gray box on the screen.

Most questions are worth 1 point. If a question is worth more than 1 point, it will have special directions that indicate how many points you can receive.

A clock at the top of the screen will show you how much time is remaining. The clock will not count down while you are listening. The clock will count down only while you are answering the questions.

AT05-01

1 What are the speakers mainly discussing?

    Ⓐ A center for students that just opened this semester

    Ⓑ The poor performances of student activity center employees

    Ⓒ Some ways to improve student morale at the school

    Ⓓ An idea the student has to improve the sharing of information

2 Why does the student tell the dean of students about her first year of college?

    Ⓐ To explain some of the hardships that she had to endure during that time

    Ⓑ To state that she nearly dropped out of school because it was so difficult

    Ⓒ To mention that it was the main reason she decided on her current major

    Ⓓ To claim that she got good grades then despite having various troubles

3 What kind of work would the employees at the student's proposed information center do?

Click on 2 answers.

    ① Support individuals who would like to start their own clubs

    ② Assist students in applying for academic scholarships

    ③ Help students get used to life on campus

    ④ Give advice on which classes students should enroll in

4   What is the student's opinion of some of the employees on campus?

Ⓐ They are happy to assist students who are in need of help.

Ⓑ They are unable to answer many questions that students ask them.

Ⓒ They are not particularly interested in doing their jobs.

Ⓓ They need to get more training to learn to do their jobs better.

5   What does the dean of students tell the student to do?

Ⓐ Schedule another appointment to meet with her next week

Ⓑ Write a formal proposal for the implementation of her idea

Ⓒ Visit some of the offices on campus and ask for assistance

Ⓓ Have her academic advisor assist her in choosing classes

Zoology

6   What aspect of termites does the professor mainly discuss?

   Click on 2 answers.

   1 The type of food that they normally consume

   2 The best ways to eradicate them from an area

   3 The places where they prefer to build their mounds

   4 The duties of various types of termites

7   Why does the professor mention tropical and subtropical regions?

   Ⓐ To claim that termite mounds in those places can be quite large

   Ⓑ To explain to the class why most termites live in those places

   Ⓒ To point out that more than 3,000 species of termites live in them

   Ⓓ To state that their hot and wet conditions are less than ideal for termites

8   According to the professor, how is a termite colony organized?

   Ⓐ All of the worker termites are led by the queen termite.

   Ⓑ There are leaders and followers that have specific chores.

   Ⓒ Worker termites lead the soldier termites while the queen lays eggs.

   Ⓓ All of the termites except the king have duties they must perform.

9 What is a likely outcome of a termite becoming an adult?

   Ⓐ It will challenge the king or queen for leadership.

   Ⓑ It will live for around two years.

   Ⓒ It will grow a set of wings.

   Ⓓ It will begin taking care of eggs.

10 How are soldier termites in most species different from worker termites?

   Ⓐ They have mandibles that are larger in size.

   Ⓑ They become a shade of white that is paler.

   Ⓒ They develop body shapes that are very different.

   Ⓓ They require greater quantities of food to eat.

11 What is the professor's opinion of termites?

   Ⓐ They often act as a keystone species in a region.

   Ⓑ They should be exterminated whenever they are found.

   Ⓒ They can get rid of a great deal of unwanted plants in forests.

   Ⓓ They can provide some advantages for their ecosystems.

AT05-03

1 Why does the student visit the professor?

    Ⓐ To submit a lab report that he wrote for the professor

    Ⓑ To ask about an assignment that he has to complete

    Ⓒ To find out when the final exam is going to be held

    Ⓓ To show the professor the results of an experiment

2 Why did the student miss class recently?

    Ⓐ He had to return to his home for personal reasons.

    Ⓑ He was ill and could not attend his classes.

    Ⓒ He preferred to spend his time outdoors instead.

    Ⓓ He had no time due to some research he was doing.

3 What is the professor's attitude toward the student?

    Ⓐ He is impressed by the student's determination to do his work.

    Ⓑ He is disappointed by the student's failure to complete his assignment.

    Ⓒ He is pleased by the way the student solves problems by himself.

    Ⓓ He is unhappy with the student interrupting him while he is busy.

HELP

OK

NEXT

VOLUME

HIDE TIME 00:10:00

4 Why does the professor tell the student about the laser?

Ⓐ To mention that he is planning to repair it soon

Ⓑ To say that it has recently been recalibrated

Ⓒ To point out that it could be a cause of the problem

Ⓓ To explain why it costs a large amount of money

5 Listen again to part of the conversation. Then answer the question.

What is the purpose of the professor's response?

Ⓐ To indicate that the student probably did something wrong

Ⓑ To ask the student to repeat what he just said

Ⓒ To have the student consider everything he did during the experiment

Ⓓ To announce that he knows exactly what the problem is

Actual Test 05 91

Marine Biology

6   What is the main topic of the lecture?

    Ⓐ The types of fish that camouflage themselves

    Ⓑ The ways that fish warn others of danger

    Ⓒ The purposes of the various colors fish have

    Ⓓ The manner in which fish eyes work

7   According to the professor, what problem do scientists have regarding the study of fish eyes?

    Ⓐ The eyes of fish are very different from those that humans have.

    Ⓑ They are not exactly sure how fish interpret the colors they see.

    Ⓒ They do not know how the positions of fish's eyes affect what they see.

    Ⓓ They have not yet accepted a unifying theory on how fish eyes work.

8   Why does the professor tell the students to look at their books?

    Ⓐ To have them compare the colorings of two different tropical fish

    Ⓑ To show them a picture of how sharks use coloring as camouflage

    Ⓒ To encourage them to look at a picture of some fish in a coral reef

    Ⓓ To have them look at a diagram breaking down the parts of a fish's eye

9　Based on the information in the lecture, indicate which reason for fish coloring the statements refer to.

Click in the correct box for each statement.

	Camouflage	Species Recognition	Warning
1 Is the reason that the lionfish is brightly colored			
2 May occur for the purpose of mating			
3 Enables some fish to save energy			
4 Explains why some fish are lightly colored on their bottom parts			

10　How does the blue damsel fish warn others of its own species when danger is approaching?

Ⓐ By changing how bright its blue stripes are

Ⓑ By using ultraviolet light to make flashes

Ⓒ By becoming a duller color of blue to hide itself

Ⓓ By creating spots on its body that other fish can see

11　Listen again to part of the lecture. Then answer the question.

What does the professor mean when she says this:

Ⓐ Fish that appear hidden to human eyes may be visible to some fish.

Ⓑ Most fish have the ability to blend in with their environments.

Ⓒ Fish are capable of seeing more colors than the human eye can.

Ⓓ Some species of fish can see more colors that other species can.

AT05-05

History

Roald Amundsen

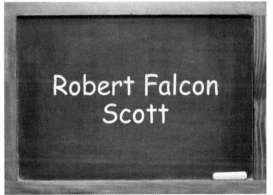

Robert Falcon Scott

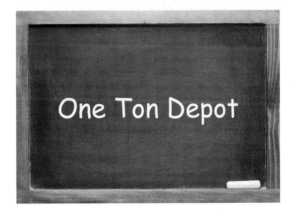

One Ton Depot

12 What is the lecture mainly about?

  (A) The reasons that Robert Falcon Scott's expedition to the South Pole failed

  (B) The race to the South Pole between Robert Falcon Scott and Roald Amundsen

  (C) What Robert Falcon Scott could have done to ensure the success of his mission

  (D) The reasons Robert Falcon Scott and Roald Amundsen went to the South Pole

13 What is the professor's opinion of Robert Falcon Scott?

  (A) He was one of the greatest explorers of the twentieth century.

  (B) He made several mistakes that he never should have made.

  (C) He was not nearly as good at exploring as was Roald Amundsen.

  (D) He knew more about Antarctica than any explorer of his day.

14 According to the professor, what was the best method for hauling sleds in Antarctica?

  (A) Having people pull their own sleds

  (B) Using teams of dogs such as huskies

  (C) Utilizing motorized vehicles

  (D) Employing ponies used to the cold

15 What was the main problem with One Ton Depot?

   Ⓐ It did not have enough supplies for replenishment.

   Ⓑ It was established in a place that was hard to reach.

   Ⓒ It took Robert Falcon Scott's team too long to set up.

   Ⓓ It was located too far away from the South Pole.

16 What comparison does the professor make between Robert Falcon Scott and Roald Amundsen?

   Ⓐ The types of animals they brought with them on their trips

   Ⓑ The troubles they encountered while going to the South Pole

   Ⓒ The fame they received upon completing their expeditions

   Ⓓ The routes that they took in order to reach the South Pole

17 How is the lecture organized?

   Ⓐ The professor switches back and forth between discussing two separate expeditions.

   Ⓑ The professor discusses the problems that occurred in reverse chronological order.

   Ⓒ The professor describes the events that happened in chronological order.

   Ⓓ The professor focuses mostly on what took place after the failure of the expedition.

Actual Test

\

06

Listening Section Directions

This section measures your ability to understand conversations and lectures in English.

The Listening section is divided into separately timed parts. In each part, you will listen to 1 conversation and 1 or 2 lectures. You will hear each conversation or lecture only one time.

After each conversation or lecture, you will answer some questions about it. The questions typically ask about the main idea and supporting details. Some questions ask about a speaker's purpose or attitude. Answer the questions based on what is stated or implied by the speakers.

You may take notes while you listen. You may use your notes to help you answer the questions. Your notes will not be scored.

If you need to change the volume while you listen, click on the **VOLUME ICON** at the top of the screen.

In some questions, you will see this icon: 🎧 This means that you will hear, but not see, part of the question.

Some of the questions have special directions. These directions appear in a gray box on the screen.

Most questions are worth 1 point. If a question is worth more than 1 point, it will have special directions that indicate how many points you can receive.

A clock at the top of the screen will show you how much time is remaining. The clock will not count down while you are listening. The clock will count down only while you are answering the questions.

AT06-01

1 Why does the student visit the dining services office?

   (A) To ask why there are no trays in the dining hall

   (B) To change the meal ticket she bought for the semester

   (C) To complain about the quality of the food at lunch

   (D) To praise the dining services for being environmentally conscious

2 According to the student, what happened at the dining hall when she had lunch?

   (A) She dropped a bowl of food on the floor.

   (B) She saw someone spill his drink on himself.

   (C) She found a tray after looking for a long time.

   (D) She knocked over a bowl of soup while she was eating.

3 In the conversation, the student describes a number of facts about what she intends to do regarding the dining service's new policy. Indicate whether each of the following is a fact or not.

   Click in the correct box for each statement.

	Fact	Not a Fact
1 She is going to set up an appointment with the school president.		
2 She will organize a petition to object to the change at the dining halls.		
3 She will encourage some other students to join her in protesting.		
4 She will encourage the dining services employees to go on strike.		

4   What can be inferred about the dining services employee?

   Ⓐ She is annoyed by all of the questions that the student is asking.

   Ⓑ She intends to help the student organize some protests against the school.

   Ⓒ She will return the operations of the dining services to normal next week.

   Ⓓ She disapproves of how the president's decision has affected the dining halls.

5   Listen again to part of the conversation. Then answer the question.

Why does the student say this:

   Ⓐ To express her desire to help the environment as much as possible

   Ⓑ To reiterate that she saw many students break items in the dining hall

   Ⓒ To indicate that the new policy will be a waste of money for the school

   Ⓓ To stress her desire to come to an agreement with the woman

AT06-02

Botany

tundra

permafrost

Arctic moss

Arctic willow

bearberry

diamond leaf willow

6   What comparison does the professor make between the summer and winter months in the Arctic?

    Ⓐ The average temperature during each period

    Ⓑ The amount of sunlight that the region gets

    Ⓒ The number of days that it snows then

    Ⓓ The wind conditions during each of these times

7   In the lecture, the professor describes a number of facts about the plants that grow in the Arctic. Indicate whether each of the following is a fact or not.

Click in the correct box for each statement.

	Fact	Not a Fact
1 Their roots are able to grow into the permafrost.		
2 They mostly grow very low to the ground.		
3 They grow close to one another.		
4 They have leaves that are long and broad.		

8   According to the professor, what is one way that Arctic moss affects the tundra?

    Ⓐ It grows so thickly that it helps warm the land beneath it.

    Ⓑ It retains a large amount of water that some animals drink.

    Ⓒ It produces berries that can be eaten by many animals.

    Ⓓ It provides nutrients for the soil, so it helps other plants grow well.

9   Why does the professor mention the Inuit people?

  Ⓐ To explain how they can survive the harsh weather in the Arctic

  Ⓑ To state that they highly value a certain plant growing in the Arctic

  Ⓒ To note that they try to avoid living in places that have tundra

  Ⓓ To claim that they often eat the fruit of the bearberry plant

10 What will the professor probably do next?

  Ⓐ Show a picture to the students and talk about it

  Ⓑ Allow the students to take a short break

  Ⓒ Ask the students about some plants growing in the Arctic

  Ⓓ Assign a homework project to the students

11 Listen again to part of the lecture. Then answer the question.

  What does the professor mean when she says this:

  Ⓐ Arctic plants are not able to get enough sunlight to grow well.

  Ⓑ There are virtually no plants of note that grow in the Arctic.

  Ⓒ The conditions in the Arctic are not good for most plants to grow.

  Ⓓ The cold weather kills the vast majority of plants living in the Arctic.

AT06-03

Chemistry

12 What is the lecture mainly about?

    Ⓐ Why so many elements were discovered during the 1700s

    Ⓑ What the characteristics of hydrogen, nitrogen, and oxygen are

    Ⓒ How people used scientific methods to discover some elements

    Ⓓ When the majority of elements on the periodic table were identified

13 Why does the professor mention Robert Boyle?

    Ⓐ To state that he discovered hydrogen but did not realize it

    Ⓑ To explain what Boyle's Law is and how he came up with it

    Ⓒ To discuss all of his contributions to the field of chemistry

    Ⓓ To claim that he taught a number of scientists in the 1600s

14 Who discovered nitrogen?

    Ⓐ Jean-Antoine Chaptal

    Ⓑ Daniel Rutherford

    Ⓒ Antoine Lavoisier

    Ⓓ Carl Wilhelm Scheele

15 Based on the information in the lecture, indicate which element the statements refer to.

Click in the correct box for each statement.

	Hydrogen	Oxygen
1 Was discovered by Henry Cavendish		
2 Was first given the name inflammable air		
3 Was found in experiments involving heated metals		
4 Was known to make flames burn intensely		

16 Why does the professor tell the class about the experiments conducted by Carl Wilhelm Scheele?

Ⓐ To compare his methods with those of Cavendish

Ⓑ To respond to an inquiry by a student

Ⓒ To point out a problem with his work

Ⓓ To show how they related to the phlogiston theory

17 How does the professor organize the information about elements that he presents to the class?

Ⓐ He talks about the discovery of three elements in reverse chronological order.

Ⓑ He provides biographies of the scientists who found each of the elements.

Ⓒ He discusses the three elements that he considers to be the most important.

Ⓓ He covers three separate elements by describing each of them individually.

1 Why did the student visit the professor?

   Ⓐ To request that the professor go over a term paper he wrote

   Ⓑ To ask the professor to clarify a comment he made in class

   Ⓒ To find out what information will be on an upcoming exam

   Ⓓ To seek permission to write an essay on Rome for bonus points

2 What can be inferred about the student?

   Ⓐ He is currently in his freshman year of college.

   Ⓑ He wants the professor to be his academic advisor.

   Ⓒ He plans to take another history class next semester.

   Ⓓ He was not a diligent student in high school.

3 Why does the professor ask the student about the Roman Empire?

   Ⓐ To find out why the student wants to know more about it

   Ⓑ To see if the student is interested in becoming a history major

   Ⓒ To determine the amount of knowledge the student has

   Ⓓ To find out how well the student will do on the next test

4   According to the professor, what did the Byzantine Empire do?

   Click on 2 answers.

   1 It helped the people of Europe remain safe from invaders.

   2 It fought Western invaders to keep Rome safe.

   3 It saved knowledge that was learned in ancient times.

   4 It trained many scholars during the Renaissance.

5   What will the student probably do next?

   Ⓐ Give the professor a paper to look over

   Ⓑ Go to a classroom to attend a class

   Ⓒ Check out some books at the library

   Ⓓ Ask the professor another question

AT06-05

Art History

Mary Cassatt

6   What aspect of Mary Cassatt does the professor mainly discuss?

  Ⓐ The difficult relationship that she had with her parents

  Ⓑ The reason that she decided to become an artist

  Ⓒ The styles of art that she painted during her lifetime

  Ⓓ The effects that Edgar Degas and other artists had on her

7   What is the professor's opinion of Mary Cassatt's art?

  Ⓐ It should be rated more highly than it presently is.

  Ⓑ It was some of the best that was painted in the 1800s.

  Ⓒ It lacked skill since she often changed her style.

  Ⓓ It was at its best when she was creating Romantic art.

8   According to the professor, what was the importance of *A Mandolin Player*?

  Ⓐ It was the first piece of art that Mary Cassatt ever sold.

  Ⓑ It proved that Mary Cassatt was an outstanding Impressionist artist.

  Ⓒ It attracted the attention of many famous artists of Mary Cassatt's time.

  Ⓓ It was selected to be presented at a prestigious exhibition.

9   In the lecture, the professor describes a number of facts about Mary Cassatt. Indicate whether each of the following is a fact or not.

Click in the correct box for each statement.

	Fact	Not a Fact
① Her desire to paint professionally was opposed by her parents.		
② She painted in both the Romantic and Impressionist styles.		
③ She never lacked funds since she sold numerous paintings during her life.		
④ She did not create any art during the last decade of her life.		

10   What does the professor imply about Edgar Degas?

    Ⓐ He played a role in Mary Cassatt becoming a member of the Impressionist Movement.

    Ⓑ It was thanks to him that Mary Cassatt's work was displayed by the Paris Salon.

    Ⓒ His assistance enabled Mary Cassatt to become a better drawer than painter.

    Ⓓ He became one of Mary Cassatt's closest friends while she was living in Europe.

11   Listen again to part of the lecture. Then answer the question.

What is the purpose of the professor's response?

    Ⓐ To provide the name of the artist she is going to discuss

    Ⓑ To say that the student's analysis of the painting is wrong

    Ⓒ To encourage the student to attempt another guess

    Ⓓ To indicate that the student provided an incorrect answer

Actual Test

07

Listening Section Directions

This section measures your ability to understand conversations and lectures in English.

The Listening section is divided into separately timed parts. In each part, you will listen to 1 conversation and 1 or 2 lectures. You will hear each conversation or lecture only one time.

After each conversation or lecture, you will answer some questions about it. The questions typically ask about the main idea and supporting details. Some questions ask about a speaker's purpose or attitude. Answer the questions based on what is stated or implied by the speakers.

You may take notes while you listen. You may use your notes to help you answer the questions. Your notes will not be scored.

If you need to change the volume while you listen, click on the **VOLUME ICON** at the top of the screen.

In some questions, you will see this icon: 🎧 This means that you will hear, but not see, part of the question.

Some of the questions have special directions. These directions appear in a gray box on the screen.

Most questions are worth 1 point. If a question is worth more than 1 point, it will have special directions that indicate how many points you can receive.

A clock at the top of the screen will show you how much time is remaining. The clock will not count down while you are listening. The clock will count down only while you are answering the questions.

sexual dimorphism

the orchid mantis

1   What are the speakers mainly discussing?

   (A) A presentation which the student recently made

   (B) A possible topic for the student to speak about in class

   (C) An outline the student turned in to the professor

   (D) A research paper the student will give a presentation on

2   Why does the professor tell the student about the bird of paradise?

   (A) To encourage her to add it to her presentation

   (B) To point out that her thoughts on it are incorrect

   (C) To say that males are less colorful than females

   (D) To ask her to explain why she plans to discuss it

3   What is the professor's opinion of the student's theory on sexual dimorphism?

   (A) She clearly understands all aspects of the topic.

   (B) She is completely wrong about why it exists for animals.

   (C) She has a limited understanding of its causes and effects.

   (D) She has an incorrect opinion about one aspect of it.

4   According to the professor, what is a result of the size of the female orchid mantis?

Click on 2 answers.

1 It is able to hunt some small mammals and birds at times.

2 It often kills and eats male mantises after it mates with them.

3 It must eat a lot more than males of the species.

4 It behaves in a more aggressive ways than males do.

5   What is the likely outcome of the student reading the magazine article the professor recommends?

A She will ask the professor to explain one of the theories mentioned in it.

B She will learn about some examples she can use for her presentation.

C She will decide to change the topic that she is going to talk about.

D She will realize that she needs to remove some animals from her presentation.

AT07-02

Musicology

the jukebox

6   Why does the professor tell the students about the mechanical piano player?

   Ⓐ To point out that it was invented by Thomas Edison

   Ⓑ To name one of the machines that the jukebox developed from

   Ⓒ To describe some of the faults that the machine had

   Ⓓ To talk about its popularity in comparison with that of the jukebox

7   Why does the professor discuss RCA?

   Ⓐ To explain how its business model made use of jukeboxes

   Ⓑ To describe the features on the jukeboxes it manufactured

   Ⓒ To mention how much it profited thanks to the jukebox

   Ⓓ To say that it published music by Elvis Presley and the Beatles

8   Based on the information in the lecture, indicate whether the statements refer to causes or effects of the popularity of the jukebox.

   Click in the correct box for each statement.

	Cause	Effect
① Fewer people listened to the radio.		
② People wanted to hear certain songs.		
③ Individuals frequently left their homes to listen to music.		
④ Advertisers spent less money at radio stations.		

9   What is the professor's opinion of the jukebox?

    Ⓐ It was responsible for changing American culture in the 1960s.

    Ⓑ It was the driving force behind the popularity of rock music.

    Ⓒ It was effective at making money for people in the music industry.

    Ⓓ It was a nice fad but was not nearly the equal of the radio.

10 What will the professor probably do next?

    Ⓐ Answer the student's question

    Ⓑ Let the students take a short break

    Ⓒ Start talking about a new topic

    Ⓓ Have the class listen to some music

11 Listen again to part of the lecture. Then answer the question.

    What can be inferred about the student when he says this:

    Ⓐ He has watched a large number of classic movies.

    Ⓑ He believes 45s produce low-quality music.

    Ⓒ He is eager to hear some music on a 45.

    Ⓓ He has never played a vinyl record before.

AT07-03

1 Why does the student visit the professor?

    Ⓐ To ask him if he is going to hire any interns this summer

    Ⓑ To request that he hire her as an assistant during vacation

    Ⓒ To inquire about his plans for the upcoming summer vacation

    Ⓓ To discuss the possibility of getting a summer internship

2 According to the student, what did she do during her previous summer vacations?

   Click on 2 answers.

    ☐1 She attended classes at the school.

    ☐2 She tutored some high school students in her major.

    ☐3 She attained part-time employment on campus.

    ☐4 She went to her hometown and worked there.

3 Why does the student ask the professor about his prior employment in the business sector?

    Ⓐ To question him about his experience in the business world

    Ⓑ To find out if he still keeps in touch with people he knew then

    Ⓒ To determine what type of work he used to do in the past

    Ⓓ To ask him if he knows a person whose company she is applying to

4   What is the professor's opinion of the student?

    Ⓐ She could become a straight-A student by studying harder.

    Ⓑ She is being selfish by taking up too much of his time.

    Ⓒ She should not ask him to favor her over the other students.

    Ⓓ She deserves to be selected for an internship by a company.

5   Listen again to part of the conversation. Then answer the question.

Why does the professor say this:

    Ⓐ To indicate that he already knows about several companies that need interns

    Ⓑ To state his desire to give all of his students the same chance for an internship

    Ⓒ To admonish the student for asking him to give her special treatment

    Ⓓ To point out that other students have asked him about available internships

AT07-04

Physiology

6   What is the likely outcome of a person eating a large amount of simple sugars?

Ⓐ The individual will become lactose intolerant.

Ⓑ The individual will come down with diabetes.

Ⓒ The individual will begin to lose weight.

Ⓓ The individual will feel energetic all day long.

7   According to the professor, which type of food contains starch?

Click on 2 answers.

1 Lettuce

2 Kale

3 Peas

4 Beans

8   Based on the information in the lecture, indicate which type of carbohydrates the statements refer to.

Click in the correct box for each statement.

	Sugar	Starch	Fiber
1 Is a complex carbohydrate found in whole grains			
2 Can help the body with digestion			
3 Includes both fructose and lactose			
4 Is often found in leafy green vegetables			

9   What does the professor imply about the modern-day health crisis?

    Ⓐ It was started by the actions of food-processing companies.

    Ⓑ It can be overcome if people eat more fiber and less sugar and starch.

    Ⓒ It is causing the cost of basic health care to increase for most people.

    Ⓓ It has resulted in more health problems than any other issue.

10   How does the professor organize the information about carbohydrates that she presents to the class?

    Ⓐ By discussing the various types of carbohydrates that exist one at a time

    Ⓑ By focusing first on the similarities between the carbohydrates and then on the differences

    Ⓒ By naming some foods and then talking about the carbohydrates contained in them

    Ⓓ By first talking about complex carbohydrates and then covering simple ones

11   Listen again to part of the lecture. Then answer the question.

    Why does the professor say this:

    Ⓐ To explain her previous statement

    Ⓑ To talk about a common problem

    Ⓒ To give the students some advice

    Ⓓ To discuss a well-known theory

AT07-05

History of Technology

androids vs. cyborgs

R2-D2 and C3PO ©Krikkiat

Lieutenant Commander Data

12 What is the main topic of the lecture?

    (A) The advances humans have made in android and cyborg technology

    (B) The similarities and differences between androids and cyborgs

    (C) The origins of the terms robot, android, and cyborg

    (D) The way that science fiction has made use of androids and cyborgs

13 Why does the professor mention Karel Capek?

    (A) To credit him with inventing the term robot

    (B) To discuss his role in science-fiction literature

    (C) To talk about how he used android technology

    (D) To go over the plot of a play that he wrote

14 According to the professor, what mistake was made in *Star Wars*?

    (A) R2-D2 and C3PO used artificial intelligence that does not exist.

    (B) Some of the androids too closely resembled humans in appearance.

    (C) The wrong word was used to refer to some of the robots.

    (D) The machines were called androids when they were actually cyborgs.

15 Based on the information in the lecture, indicate which type of machine the statements refer to.

Click in the correct box for each statement.

	Android	Cyborg
1 Contains some mechanical elements in an organic body		
2 Could be either a person or an animal		
3 Was first used as a term in the nineteenth century		
4 Is a machine that resembles humans in action and appearance		

16 What will the professor probably do next?

(A) Show a film about the history of robots

(B) Continue to lecture to the class on cyborgs

(C) Give a study sheet to the students

(D) Wait for a student to answer his question

17 Listen again to part of the lecture. Then answer the question.

Why does the professor say this:

(A) To emphasize a point that he is making

(B) To give his opinion on a certain matter

(C) To correct a mistake he just made

(D) To provide a definition of a crucial term

Actual Test

08

Listening Section Directions

This section measures your ability to understand conversations and lectures in English.

The Listening section is divided into separately timed parts. In each part, you will listen to 1 conversation and 1 or 2 lectures. You will hear each conversation or lecture only one time.

After each conversation or lecture, you will answer some questions about it. The questions typically ask about the main idea and supporting details. Some questions ask about a speaker's purpose or attitude. Answer the questions based on what is stated or implied by the speakers.

You may take notes while you listen. You may use your notes to help you answer the questions. Your notes will not be scored.

If you need to change the volume while you listen, click on the **VOLUME ICON** at the top of the screen.

In some questions, you will see this icon: 🎧 This means that you will hear, but not see, part of the question.

Some of the questions have special directions. These directions appear in a gray box on the screen.

Most questions are worth 1 point. If a question is worth more than 1 point, it will have special directions that indicate how many points you can receive.

A clock at the top of the screen will show you how much time is remaining. The clock will not count down while you are listening. The clock will count down only while you are answering the questions.

AT08-01

1 What are the speakers mainly discussing?

    Ⓐ The rules that must be followed during the school's quiet period

    Ⓑ The upcoming final exam period and how they are going to study

    Ⓒ Some students in their dormitory who have been disturbing others

    Ⓓ The opinions of some of the other students living on their floor

2 What is the student's opinion of Terry and Paul?

    Ⓐ He considers them to be good friends.

    Ⓑ He thinks they are too argumentative.

    Ⓒ He dislikes how they act during the day.

    Ⓓ He believes they make too much noise.

3 What can be inferred about the resident assistant?

    Ⓐ He does not want the students to file a complaint with the student housing office.

    Ⓑ He spends most of his time at the library, so is rarely in the dormitory.

    Ⓒ He is close friends with Terry and Paul, so he ignores the problems they cause.

    Ⓓ He acts sternly toward students who live on his floor and make problems for others.

4 What will the resident assistant probably do next?

  Ⓐ Visit the student housing office

  Ⓑ File a complaint against the student

  Ⓒ Go to speak with Terry and Paul

  Ⓓ Return to his room in order to study

5 Listen again to part of the conversation. Then answer the question.

Why does the student say this:

  Ⓐ To express his disbelief at the resident assistant's comment

  Ⓑ To show that he is in full agreement with the resident assistant

  Ⓒ To indicate his anger with some of the students on his floor

  Ⓓ To prove that the resident assistant has not been doing his job properly

🎧 AT08-02

American
Literature

6   What aspect of Mark Twain does the professor mainly discuss?

    Ⓐ The effect that the Realist Movement had on his work

    Ⓑ Some of the important events that happened in his life

    Ⓒ The popularity of his novels in the nineteenth century

    Ⓓ Some of the jobs that he did before he became a novelist

7   Why does the professor tell the students about the time Mark Twain spent working on a riverboat?

    Ⓐ To name the first job he ever had

    Ⓑ To talk about his love for the Mississippi River

    Ⓒ To discuss riverboat culture with the class

    Ⓓ To explain the origin of his penname

8   According to the professor, what was Mark Twain's first success as a writer?

    Ⓐ *The Adventures of Tom Sawyer*

    Ⓑ *The Adventures of Huckleberry Finn*

    Ⓒ "The Celebrated Jumping Frog of Calaveras County"

    Ⓓ *Innocents Abroad*

9 What is the professor's attitude toward the language Mark Twain used in *The Adventures of Huckleberry Finn*?

(A) Its usage of colloquialisms can be highly entertaining.

(B) She dislikes the fact that it can be hard to understand.

(C) It has prevented many people from fully enjoying his work.

(D) His writing contained too many made-up expressions.

10 What caused writers in the 1800s to begin using colloquial language in their works?

(A) A desire to make their writing appeal to the upper class

(B) An urge to record the language spoken by regular Americans

(C) The rising popularity of novels with realistic characters

(D) An increase in the mass education of common people

11 Listen again to part of the lecture. Then answer the question.

What does the professor imply when she says this:

(A) She assigned the students to read *The Adventures of Huckleberry Finn*.

(B) She hopes that the reports the students submit will be insightful.

(C) She thinks *The Adventures of Tom Sawyer* is Mark Twain's best book.

(D) She has a list of questions about Mark Twain's books that she will ask the students.

AT08-03

Archaeology

12 What is the main topic of the lecture?

    (A) The importance of dig sites located in urban centers

    (B) The need to record everything that is done at a dig site

    (C) The steps archaeologists follow when excavating sites

    (D) The types of artifacts that may be found during excavations

13 What is a rescue excavation?

    (A) An excavation that is done as quickly as possible

    (B) An excavation that focuses on saving fragile relics

    (C) An excavation that happens in soil from several different periods

    (D) An excavation that attempts to repair damage to artifacts

14 According to the professor, how do archaeologists examine a site before they start digging?

    Click on 2 answers.

    1 By closing observing the structures existing on the surface

    2 By using radar that can show them what is under the ground

    3 By stripping away the top layer of soil to look at the ground underneath

    4 By digging holes or trenches in places around the dig site

15 What is the professor's opinion of archaeologists who fail to dig carefully?

Ⓐ They should be prevented from digging at any sites.

Ⓑ They bring dishonor to the archaeological profession.

Ⓒ They should be fined and have charges filed against them.

Ⓓ They cause damage to humans' understanding of the past.

16 How does the professor organize the information about the way archaeologists dig at sites that he presents to the class?

Ⓐ By presenting a case study of a recent dig in an urban center

Ⓑ By discussing the methods in no particular order

Ⓒ By showing slides and then explaining what is happening

Ⓓ By describing the steps to be taken in the precise order

17 Listen again to part of the lecture. Then answer the question

What can be inferred about the student when he says this: 🎧

Ⓐ He wants the professor to explain the statement he just made.

Ⓑ He has firsthand experience working at an archaeological dig site.

Ⓒ He believes there are few dig sites found in urban centers.

Ⓓ He thinks that the professor is telling the class something incorrect.

AT08-04

The Woman with a Hat

The Scream

1 What are the speakers mainly discussing?

    Ⓐ The student's interest in art from the 1800s

    Ⓑ The characteristics of the Expressionist Movement

    Ⓒ A topic that the student can write her term paper on

    Ⓓ The differences between two art movements

2 What can be inferred about *The Scream*?

    Ⓐ It is considered a work of realist art by most critics.

    Ⓑ It was the first work ever made in the Expressionist Movement.

    Ⓒ It is said to be one of Edvard Munch's greatest works.

    Ⓓ It has some stylistic similarities to *The Woman with a Hat*.

3 According to the professor, what is a feature of Fauvist works?

    Click on 2 answers.

    ① They are a type of abstract art.

    ② They have colors that are both idealized and unrealistic.

    ③ They show people with alien appearances.

    ④ They depict the strong feelings of artists.

4 Why does the student tell the professor about her learning style?

    Ⓐ To express her appreciation for the professor's teaching style

    Ⓑ To explain why she had difficulty understanding his lecture

    Ⓒ To state the reason why she rarely takes notes in her classes

    Ⓓ To ask him for advice on becoming a better listener

5 What will the student probably do next?

    Ⓐ Analyze the features of a work of art the professor shows her

    Ⓑ Leave the professor's office to attend her next class

    Ⓒ Show the professor a painting that she did in her free time

    Ⓓ Discuss another avant-garde movement with the professor

AT08-05

Psychology

lucid dreaming

Keith Herne

Stephen LaBerge

6 What can be inferred about lucid dreaming?

    (A) It is something that everyone is capable of doing.

    (B) Many experts believe that it is not possible to do.

    (C) People who do it remember their dreams fully upon waking.

    (D) It only happens to people a few times a month.

7 What is the professor's opinion on the surveys about lucid dreaming that she discusses?

    (A) She thinks proper methods were followed during them.

    (B) She believes that the results do not reflect reality.

    (C) She supports the data that they produced.

    (D) She considers the questions asked in them to be flawed.

8 Why does the professor mention Keith Herne?

    (A) To express her doubt about the theories that he came up with

    (B) To praise him for his groundbreaking work on lucid dreaming

    (C) To compare the work he did with that of researchers in the 1800s

    (D) To cover his method for determining if someone is dreaming lucidly

9   In the lecture, the professor describes a number of facts about Stephen LaBerge's work regarding lucid dreaming. Indicate whether each of the following is a fact or not.

Click in the correct box for each statement.

	Fact	Not a Fact
1 He consulted with Keith Herne before he started his observations.		
2 People's brains are more active when they are dreaming lucidly.		
3 He believes people's bodies react when they suddenly realize they are lucidly dreaming.		
4 The results of his work were published in a bestselling book.		

10 According to the professor, what is important when considering if a person is dreaming lucidly?

    Ⓐ How fast the person's heart rate is

    Ⓑ How aware the person dreaming is

    Ⓒ How much the person is perspiring

    Ⓓ How well the person can describe the dream

11 Listen again to part of the lecture. Then answer the question.

What is the purpose of the professor's response?

    Ⓐ To challenge the student to answer her own question

    Ⓑ To pose a problem for the students to solve

    Ⓒ To provide an answer to the student's question

    Ⓓ To describe the way in which an experiment is conducted

AUTHORS

Michael A. Putlack
- MA in History, Tufts University, Medford, MA, USA
- Expert test developer of TOEFL, TOEIC, and TEPS
- Main author of the Darakwon *How to Master Skills for the TOEFL® iBT* series and *TOEFL® MAP* series

Stephen Poirier
- Candidate for PhD in History, University of Western Ontario, Canada
- Certificate of Professional Technical Writing, Carleton University, Canada
- Co-author of the Darakwon *How to Master Skills for the TOEFL® iBT* series and *TOEFL® MAP* series

Maximilian Tolochko
- BA in History and Education, University of Oklahoma, USA
- MS in Procurement and Contract Management, Florida Institute of Technology, USA
- Co-author of the Darakwon *TOEFL® MAP* series

Decoding the **TOEFL**® iBT
Actual Test **LISTENING** 2 NEW TOEFL® EDITION

Publisher Chung Kyudo
Editors Kim Minju, Seo Jeongah
Authors Michael A. Putlack, Stephen Poirier, Maximilian Tolochko
Proofreader Michael A. Putlack
Designers Koo Soojung, Park Sunyoung

First published in March 2020
By Darakwon, Inc.
Darakwon Bldg., 211, Munbal-ro, Paju-si, Gyeonggi-do 10881
Republic of Korea
Tel: 82-2-736-2031 (Ext. 250)
Fax: 82-2-732-2037

ISBN 978-89-277-0868-1 14740
       978-89-277-0862-9 14740 (set)

www.darakwon.co.kr

Photo Credits
Oona Raisanen (p. 35)
https://commons.wikimedia.org/wiki/File:Map_of_Franz_Josef_
Land-en.svg
Krikkiat (p. 131) / Shutterstock.com

Components Test Book / Answer Book
9 8 7 6 5 4 3   24 25 26 27 28

Decoding the
TOEFL® iBT

Answers
Scripts
Explanations

Actual Test

LISTENING 2

Decoding the TOEFL® iBT

Actual Test

LISTENING 2

Answers
Scripts
Explanations

Actual Test 01

ANSWERS

PART 1

1 Ⓑ	2 Ⓐ	3 Ⓒ	4 Ⓐ	5 Ⓓ
6 Ⓓ	7 Ⓐ	8 Ⓒ-Ⓑ-Ⓓ-Ⓐ		
9 Ⓐ	10 Ⓓ	11 Ⓑ		

PART 2

1 Ⓐ	2 Fact: ②, ③ Not a Fact: ①, ④			
3 Ⓒ	4 Ⓒ	5 Ⓒ	6 Ⓓ	7 Ⓐ
8 Ⓐ	9 Ⓒ	10 Ⓑ	11 Ⓐ	12 Ⓓ
13 Ⓐ	14 Ⓐ	15 Ⓓ	16 Ⓒ	17 Ⓒ

PART 1 Conversation

Script

Listen to part of a conversation between a student and a professor.

W Student: Good morning, Professor Hamilton. I received your email that you wanted to see me about something, so, uh, here I am.

M Professor: Good morning to you, Marilynn. Thanks for coming over so quickly. Honestly, I wasn't expecting to see you until sometime this afternoon.

W: It's not every day that one of my professors sends me an email, so I figured this must be something important. Since I've got, oh, about half an hour prior to the start of my next class, I decided to drop by your office right now.

M: I see. Well, it's nice to see you have good instincts. In fact, the reason I wanted to see you is fairly important.

W: Yeah, uh . . . your email was sort of vague about that. I'm not in any kind of trouble, am I? I mean, I didn't forget to, uh, I don't know, to turn in a homework assignment, did I?

M: Not at all, Marilynn. Don't worry about that.

W: That's a relief.

M: The reason I asked you here is that I recall a conversation we had a month or so ago. You mentioned to me that the tuition at the school was getting so high that you and your family were having a bit of trouble paying your bills.

W: Yes, I remember telling you about that.

M: Well, I have something here that might be of interest to

you. Here, uh, check out this brochure I just got in the mail this morning.

W: Hmm . . . Let me see . . . An art scholarship?

M: Yes, that's right. An art scholarship. I thought you might be interested in applying for it. If you win, your tuition would be paid for an entire academic year. Imagine that . . . You'd get free tuition for your senior year.

W: Wow . . . That would be nice. But, uh . . . Professor Hamilton, I'm really flattered you believe the art I produce is good enough to win a contest, but, um . . . I don't see it that way. There's no way I could ever win this contest. There are so many other students who create better art than I do.

M: First of all, there's no harm in trying. You can submit one of the more recent pieces you painted. I highly recommend that you submit the landscape you painted a couple of weeks ago. 🎧4You know which one I'm referring to, right? It's the one you did of the lake.

W: You think that one's worthy enough to enter in the contest? Seriously?

M: Honestly, I think you're selling yourself short concerning your artistic abilities. That landscape is easily the best one produced by any of my students this year. Marilynn, you are exceptionally talented at painting even if you don't want to admit it.

W: Er . . . I don't know. I've never had anyone compliment my art like that before. I, uh, I don't know what to say.

M: 🎧5Well, um, I believe you have an outstanding chance of winning. **And even if you don't win, the second and third place prizes are still nice and would help you with your tuition as well.** Why don't we look at this together and figure out how you can enter the contest?

W: Do you have time to do that now?

M: Sure. It shouldn't take too long. We can go over everything before you have to attend your next class.

Answer Explanations

1 Gist-Purpose Question

Ⓑ The professor says, "The reason I asked you here is that I recall a conversation we had a month or so ago. You mentioned to me that the tuition at the school was getting so high that you and your family were having a bit of trouble paying your bills." Then, he tells the student about the upcoming art contest.

2 Making Inferences Question

Ⓐ The professor tells the student, "I thought you might

be interested in applying for it. If you win, your tuition would be paid for an entire academic year. Imagine that . . . You'd get free tuition for your senior year." It can therefore be inferred that the student is currently a junior.

3 Making Inferences Question

Ⓒ At the end of the conversation, the professor suggests, "Why don't we look at this together and figure out how you can enter the contest?" and the student agrees with his suggestion.

4 Understanding Attitude Question

Ⓐ When the professor says, "You're selling yourself short concerning your artistic abilities," he means that the student is skilled as an artist even though she might not think so.

5 Understanding Function Question

Ⓓ When the professor says that the second and third places awards are nice and that they "would help you with your tuition as well," he is implying that they are cash awards.

PART 1 Lecture

Script

Listen to part of a lecture in an art history class.

M Professor: Etching is another way to make illustrations for paper prints. It's widely believed to have evolved either from the goldsmith trade or from armorers. In both trades, craftsmen engraved elaborate designs in gold or metal armor. Etching also might have been used in ancient times, but nobody's positive about that. What we are certain about, however, is that the using of metal plates with designs on them in order to make prints on paper developed during the early sixteenth century in either Italy or Germany. But before we dive into the history of etching, I think it would be best if I explained the process first.

Here's what happens . . . First, the artist coats some kind of a metal surface—normally copper—with wax or some other acid-resistant substance. Next, the artist cuts into the wax with sharp tools to make the desired design. Sometimes the design is drawn on paper first, and then the paper is laid on top of the wax. But, depending upon the artist, that doesn't always happen. Anyway, once the wax is cut, the metal plate with the wax coating is dipped in an acid bath. We call the acid a mordant. The acid eats away, or bites, the metal in the places where the wax was removed. Each time the acid works on a metal plate is called a biting. Oh, and just so you know, some artists use a single biting while

others use more than one biting on a single work. Once the acid does its job, the wax is removed from the plate and the plate is coated in ink. The ink is subsequently wiped from the surface of the plate, which leaves the ink in the deep lines that the acid bit into the metal plate. After that, the metal plate is put in a printing press, paper is pressed against the plate, and an image is printed. Finally, the paper is removed and hung up to dry much like wet clothes on a clothesline.

Although there are variations on this method, those are the basic steps involved. The resulting image is called an etching, and, um, the process is also called etching. When it was developed in the sixteenth century, there were several advantages to this technique. First, it permitted many copies of a single etching to be made. This benefitted book publishers in the early days of the printing press. Prior to that, pictures in books had to be done by hand or by printing designs carved in wooden blocks, which was a slow process that didn't produce a lot of copies. A second advantage was that artists could produce multiple copies of their works and sell them all, which benefitted the artists financially. A third advantage was that once the initial etching was made on the metal plate, it could be added to, which, uh, which allowed artists to create better designs and to improve upon their work.

Um, let me say a few words about the history of etching and some famous artists who used that technique. Again, as I already mentioned, there's some uncertainty about where it first developed. Some art historians believe it was pioneered in Northern Italy in the late fifteenth century, but I've got my doubts about that. What is not in doubt, however, is where the earliest examples of etchings made for the printing industry came from. They were done by an armorer named Daniel Hopfer in Augsburg, Germany, in the early sixteenth century. Hopfer worked on iron plates just like he did when making armor. Later, it was discovered that copper was easier to work with because the acid more readily bit into it.

Of the numerous artists who have made extensive use of etchings, arguably the most famous is Rembrandt. During his lifetime, he achieved more fame for his etchings than for his paintings—rightfully so as some of his etchings are simply incredible. I believe the reason people knew his etchings better is that, well, there was merely a single copy of each of his paintings. So they were viewed by relatively few people while he was alive. On the other hand, multiple copies of his etchings were made, so more people saw them, and they even appeared in books and broadsheets that were widely published, which enabled the public to see them much more than his paintings.

Actual Test 01　**3**

So what about Rembrandt and his etchings . . . ? Oh, in case you aren't aware, he was from the Netherlands and lived from 1606 to 1669. He's widely considered a master of etching. In fact, his skill was so great that many people thought he had devised some new techniques. A close examination of both his life and work has revealed that Rembrandt had no secret other than his talent though. Oh, yes, and his patience. You see, he frequently reworked his etchings by adding different aspects to them until he was fully satisfied. As for the subject matter of his etchings, well, he did lots of things . . . landscapes, portraits, nudes, and even scenes from the Bible. Let's take a look at some of his more famous ones now.

Answer Explanations

6 Gist-Content Question

(D) The professor mostly tells the students about the early history of etching and also explains how it is done.

7 Understanding Organization Question

(A) When talking about Daniel Hopfer, the professor focuses on the historical importance of the etching work that he did.

8 Connecting Content Question

Order: (C) – (B) – (D) – (A)

About etching, the professor says, "First, the artist coats some kind of a metal surface—normally copper—with wax or some other acid-resistant substance. Next, the artist cuts into the wax with sharp tools to make the desired design. Sometimes the design is drawn on paper first, and then the paper is laid on top of the wax. But, depending upon the artist, that doesn't always happen. Anyway, once the wax is cut, the metal plate with the wax coating is dipped in an acid bath. We call the acid a mordant. The acid eats away, or bites, the metal in the places where the wax was removed. Each time the acid works on a metal plate is called a biting. Oh, and just so you know, some artists use a single biting while others use more than one biting on a single work. Once the acid does its job, the wax is removed from the plate and the plate is coated in ink."

9 Understanding Attitude Question

(A) About Rembrandt's etchings, the professor declares, "During his lifetime, he achieved more fame for his etchings than for his paintings—rightfully so as some of his etchings are simply incredible."

10 Connecting Content Question

(D) The professor says about Rembrandt, "You see,

he frequently reworked his etchings by adding different aspects to them until he was fully satisfied." Earlier in the lecture, he noted the etchers can change their works by doing additional bitings. So it can be inferred that Rembrandt made multiple bitings of many of his etchings.

11 Making Inferences Question

(B) At the end of the lecture, the professor tells the class, "Let's take a look at some of his more famous ones now." So he will probably show the class some pictures.

PART 2 Conversation   p. 17

Script

Listen to part of a conversation between a student and a coach.

M1 Coach: Rick, you're just the man I wanted to see. How are you feeling today? Are you ready for the big tournament in Anniston this Saturday?

M2 Student: Uh, Coach Young, I need to tell you something important . . .

M1: What? You're not injured, are you?

M2: I feel fine, Coach, but, um . . . I have a job interview this Saturday.

M1: Oh, that's nothing. Just call the company and tell them you want to interview some other day.

M2: Actually, I already mentioned that, but, uh, apparently, I'm going to be interviewed by a team of five people, and Saturday is the only day everyone can get together to interview me. This interview is for a position I really want, Coach, so I can't skip it. But I don't want to let the team down by missing the tournament.

M1: Okay, okay . . . Slow down a bit. Let's try to figure this problem out. When and where is your interview supposed to be?

M2: I have to be at the company's office in Oxford by eleven o'clock. The person I spoke with told me that most interviews of this nature take about two hours to conclude.

M1: Hmm . . . So that means your interview should end at roughly one in the afternoon.

M2: That sounds about right.

M1: 🎧5 Well, Oxford isn't too far away from Anniston, so, uh, once you're done with the interview, just drive over to the site of the tournament. Our first game isn't scheduled to start until two in the afternoon, so I'd say you should make it there in time for tipoff.

M2: Er . . . Coach Young, I don't own a car, so I'm going to be taking the bus to get there. I checked the bus schedule, and, um . . . the first bus from Oxford to Anniston that leaves after my interview finishes isn't going to depart until a quarter to two, so I probably won't make it to the arena until three or so. It looks like you're going to have to start Don or Clark in my place. With luck, I can make it there for the second half.

M1: I don't like the sound of that. Neither Don nor Clark plays good defense, and we need our best defensive players on the court at the start of the game. Is there any way you can borrow a car from one of your friends?

M2: I've asked, but everyone I know is going to be busy.

M1: Okay, I've got an idea. I'm going to have Coach Patterson drive you to the interview. He can wait for you while you're talking to everyone at the company, and then he'll drive you to the tournament site. That way, you won't miss any of the action.

M2: Do you think Coach Patterson will mind doing that?

M1: Not at all. He's an assistant coach, so he always gets to do odd things like that. Don't be concerned about him though. I'm sure he'll volunteer to do that once I inform him of your situation.

M2: All right. Thanks a lot, Coach. I appreciate everything you're doing for me. Should I go to the locker room and change for practice?

M1: You bet. We're already five minutes late, and I've got a few things to teach you all about basketball today. Get going. I'll see you out on the court.

Answer Explanations

1 **Gist-Content Question**

Ⓐ The student has an interview on Saturday, but that is going to conflict with a basketball tournament he is supposed to play in.

2 **Detail Question**

Fact: ②, ③   Not a Fact: ①, ④

First, the student mentions, "I'm going to be interviewed by a team of five people." He further states, "I have to be at the company's office in Oxford by eleven o'clock." He does not, however, mention anything about the position being related to his major. And the interview is going to take place in Oxford, not in Anniston.

3 **Understanding Function Question**

Ⓒ About Coach Patterson, the coach comments, "I'm going to have Coach Patterson drive you to the interview. He can wait for you while you're talking to everyone at the company, and then he'll drive you to the tournament site. That way, you won't miss any of the action." So he is explaining how he will use Coach Patterson to handle the student's problem.

4 **Connecting Content Question**

Ⓒ The student says, "It looks like you're going to have to start Don or Clark in my place." And the coach says, "Neither Don nor Clark plays good defense, and we need our best defensive players on the court at the start of the game." So both of them imply that the student is a starter on the basketball team.

5 **Understanding Function Question**

Ⓒ The coach tells the student to drive to the site of the game after the interview, but the student responds that he does not have a car, so he will take the bus. In saying that, he is rejecting the coach's suggestion.

PART 2 Lecture #1   p. 20

Script

Listen to part of a lecture in a psychology class.

W Professor: Memory is basically anything you can recall that happened to you in the past. Memories can be extremely vivid or rather fuzzy with few of the details clear to the mind. There are a number of factors which play a role in which memories you can recall. One of the strongest of these factors is emotions. How you felt at the time of an event often plays a key role in how well you can recall that particular event later on.

The first thing we should examine is why we remember certain events yet simply cannot recall others at all. For instance, uh, you in the front row . . . Ω11 What did you have for lunch yesterday?

M Student: Uh . . . A sandwich? No, that's not right. Huh . . . I'm not sure. Sorry.

W: Thanks for proving my point. I'd be willing to bet that most of you can't remember what you ate for lunch yesterday. However, hmm . . . you in the front row again . . . Can you tell me about your first day of elementary school?

M: Sure. That's easy. I attended Golden Springs Elementary School, and my homeroom teacher was Mrs. Maine. I sat next to William Bannister, and we became really good friends. Also . . .

W: Um, yes, thank you. As you can see, class, memories of certain events simply come flooding back. I'm sure most of you have extremely vivid memories of your high school graduation, your sixteenth birthday, and any accidents you may have been involved in. The reason you can't remember yesterday's lunch is that it was, well, an unremarkable event. Nothing about it stood out or resonated with you, so there's no reason for you to recall such a mundane event. On the other hand, the same is not true for the other events I mentioned. You had emotional responses to your high school graduation and sixteenth birthdays. You were probably scared when you had an accident. Emotions, you see, play a strong role in which events you can remember.

A second factor that plays a role in which memories you can recall is whether the emotional response was pleasant or unpleasant. An event that was happy and provided you with great joy—uh, your high school graduation, for instance— will be easy to remember . . . but you might not recall it in as much detail as you believe you can. In contrast, it has been proven time after time that unpleasant memories are the strongest. Think about it . . . Traumatic incidents are virtually impossible to forget. If you were bitten by a dog as a child, you might remember that for your entire life, and if you were in a car accident, that memory may remain fresh for decades as well.

A third factor is whether you experienced the event alone or as a part of a group. When we experience events by ourselves, even distressing memories may fade somewhat over time. This happens because some people might not believe you when you talk about them, and that can cause you to question what actually happened. Or perhaps you kept the event secret since you were afraid to tell anyone something so, er, shocking or terrifying. This often happens to individuals who have been emotionally or physically abused . . . Sadly, they don't tell anyone, so the memories become so fragmented or fuzzy that they begin to doubt what actually happened.

But when we experience an event as a group, a collective memory will take hold. We'll talk about the event with the other people involved, and we'll express how we felt. Here's an example . . . When I was a child, a terrible car accident happened right in front of my home. My brothers, parents, neighbors, and I all saw the event take place. Fortunately, no one died, but three people were badly injured. We all talked about the crash for years afterward, so we didn't forget it. In fact, I can still remember specific details about that summer day, and so can my brothers. National events can cause a collective emotional response that results in a collective long-term memory as well. In the United States, many elderly people can recall where they were and what they were doing when they heard that President Kennedy was assassinated in 1963. As for my generation, we all remember what we were doing when the space shuttle *Challenger* exploded in 1986.

I ought to stress that not all memories from dramatic events can be recalled with perfect accuracy. This is an issue that has long plagued police investigators. The problem is that eyewitnesses to crimes are notoriously unreliable. What happens to these individuals is that they are subjected to severe stress, which causes them to get tunnel memory. For instance, during a bank robbery, the people being robbed may focus on the robbers' weapons rather than on their faces or clothes. By concentrating on the source of the danger, these eyewitnesses miss details the police need to know. Others develop illusionary memory, in which they think they recall events accurately but, um, in reality, do not. Unfortunately, such false memories have sent innocent people to prison for crimes they didn't commit.

Answer Explanations

6   Gist-Content Question

Ⓓ During the lecture, the professor focuses on the various factors that are involved in determining which events people remember.

7   Connecting Content Question

Ⓐ The professor says, "If you were bitten by a dog as a child, you might remember that for your entire life, and if you were in a car accident, that memory may remain fresh for decades as well."

8   Detail Question

Ⓐ The professor states, "Or perhaps you kept the event secret since you were afraid to tell anyone something so, er, shocking or terrifying. This often happens to individuals who have been emotionally or physically abused . . . Sadly, they don't tell anyone, so the memories become so fragmented or fuzzy that they begin to doubt what actually happened."

9   Understanding Function Question

Ⓒ The professor provides an example of a collective memory when she tells the students about the car accident she witnessed when she was a child.

10 Detail Question

Ⓑ The professor remarks, "What happens to these individuals is that they are subjected to severe stress, which causes them to get tunnel memory. For instance, during a bank robbery, the people being robbed may focus on the robbers' weapons rather than on their faces or clothes. By concentrating on the source of the danger, these eyewitnesses miss details the police need to know."

11 Understanding Function Question

Ⓐ When the professor tells the student, "Thanks for proving my point," she implies that the student answered in a way that she had expected.

PART 2 Lecture #2

p. 23

Script

Listen to part of a lecture in a physics class.

M Professor: To get a better understanding of physics, you need to know the basics, so I'm going to spend the first day of this semester ensuring that you know the nuts and bolts of physics. The first topic I shall cover is magnetism. I'm certain you've all seen magnetism at work at least by observing either magnets or a compass. A simple explanation of magnetism is that it's a force of attraction or repulsion. It can act over a distance but isn't noticeable if the distance is too great. The basic reason magnetism exists is that some objects have a magnetic field. Every magnetic field has two poles, which we call north-seeking, or north, and south-seeking, or south, poles. Any bar magnet free to rotate on its own will align with the north and south since the Earth has a magnetic field with two such poles. Between magnetic objects, opposite poles attract while like poles repulse each other.

Since ancient times, people have noticed that certain metals possess magnetic properties. By studying the ways these metals moved and attracted and repulsed one another, people got the first hints that magnetic fields exist. Please be aware that virtually all materials have magnetic fields, but they're so weak in most materials that they're unnoticeable. Materials with strong magnetic fields are called ferromagnetic. Numerous metals are ferromagnetic, but others aren't. Copper, for instance, has a low magnetic field. On the other hand, the metal we call magnetite today but, um, which was long-called lodestone, has a high magnetic field. It was one of the first metals humans observed to possess magnetic properties. Iron is another metal with a high magnetic field and is the most common metal used in the magnets produced today.

I should also point out that magnets can be permanent or temporary. Ferromagnetic materials usually produce permanent magnets while . . . Yes? You with your hand up?

W Student: I'm sorry, sir, but what do you mean by a permanent magnet?

M: I simply mean that once an object is magnetized, it maintains its magnetic field. Conversely, temporary magnets are created by an external force, uh, such as electricity, and lose their magnetic fields when that force is removed. This is why temporary magnets are useful in a number of applications: because they're not always magnetized. So, um, I'm pretty sure many of you are wondering why magnetic fields exist . . . how we can create them . . . and how we can turn them off and on. Allow me to explain . . .

There are two ways magnetic fields can be created. Naturally occurring magnetism is the result of the magnetic properties of atoms. If you take a magnet and cut it in half, you'll get two new magnets, each of which has a north pole and a south pole. If you continue to cut the magnet in half, you'll still wind up with new magnets each time. The reason is that at the subatomic level, magnetism is being created. As you should be aware, an atom has protons and neutrons in its nucleus while electrons spin around the nucleus in what's called the electron cloud. The spinning of the electrons is what produces magnetism.

How does that occur . . . ? Well, it's a complex topic and something we're going to spend more time on later in the semester, but let me give you a brief explanation. As the electrons spin, they produce a change in the energy around the atom. This is known as the magnetic moment. The number of electrons and the way they spin around the nucleus varies from atom to atom, and so does each atom's magnetic field. Additionally, the direction the electrons spin is important for creating magnetic fields. That's why some materials produce strong magnetic fields while others produce weak ones. Basically, if two electrons in an atom spin in opposite directions, they cancel out the magnetic field each produces, therefore making the atom have virtually no magnetic field.

W: Could you give us an example, please?

M: I sure can. Helium has two electrons that spin in opposite directions. As a result, helium has virtually no magnetic field. Atoms such as helium and the materials they produce are called diamagnetic materials.

All right, uh, what about the second way to produce magnetism? Well, we can create a magnetic field by using electricity. So it's possible to take a piece of iron that's not already a magnet and turn it into one, um, at least temporarily. Iron, as I told you, has strong magnetic properties and is classified as ferromagnetic. By wrapping an electric wire around an iron bar and then shooting an electric current through the wire, the iron bar becomes magnetized. But . . . when the electricity is turned off, the iron bar is no longer a magnet. This electromagnet, as we call it, is the result of the force of electricity acting on the atoms in the iron. Let's examine how that works in more detail . . .

Answer Explanations

12 Making Inferences Question

(D) The professor says, "I'm going to spend the first day of this semester ensuring that you know the nuts and bolts of physics. The first topic I shall cover is magnetism." It can therefore be inferred that the professor will talk about topics other than magnetism during the class.

13 Connecting Content Question

(A) The professor points out the strengths of the magnetic fields of the two elements.

14 Understanding Attitude Question

(A) The professor states, "This is why temporary magnets are useful in a number of applications: because they're not always magnetized."

15 Detail Question

(D) The professor tells the students, "Additionally, the direction the electrons spin is important for creating magnetic fields. That's why some materials produce strong magnetic fields while others produce weak ones."

16 Understanding Organization Question

(C) The student asks the professor to give them an example, so he talks about how helium lacks a magnetic field.

17 Making Inferences Question

(C) At the end of the lecture, the professor comments, "This electromagnet, as we call it, is the result of the force of electricity acting on the atoms in the iron. Let's examine how that works in more detail." So he will probably speak about electromagnets next.

Actual Test 02

ANSWERS

PART 1

1 (D)	2 (B)	3 (C)	4 [2], [4]	5 (A)
6 (B)	7 (A)	8 [3], [4]	9 (B)	10 (D)
11 (A)	12 (C)	13 (A)	14 [2], [3]	
15 (A)	16 (C)	17 (D)		

PART 2

1 (D)	2 (B)	3 (B)	4 [2], [3]	5 (A)
6 (C)	7 (A)	8 (B)	9 (C)	10 (C)
11 (A)				

PART 1 Conversation

p. 29

Script

Listen to part of a conversation between a student and a student housing office employee.

W Student: Excuse me, but I found this notice here attached to the door of my dorm room today. According to it, I'm supposed to report to the student housing office at once. Er . . . Can you tell me what this is all about?

M Student Housing Office Employee: Could I please see the note? I need to take a look at it before I can tell you why someone requested that you visit us.

W: Sure. Here you are . . .

M: Thank you. Just a minute . . . Hmm . . . I need to check a file on my computer here. Would you mind waiting a moment, please?

W: Go ahead.

M: Thanks . . . Okay, I see what the problem is. First, let me confirm. Your name is Jennifer Wellman?

W: That's correct.

M: And you currently reside in a single room in Felton Hall?

W: Yes, that's right. I live in room 507. Look, um, can you tell me what's going on? I have a class to attend fifteen minutes from now, and it's practically on the other side of campus. I don't have much time to stay here.

M: I understand. Then let me get straight to the point. You were cited for removing some furniture from your room and then placing it in the hall.

W: Huh? Furniture? I didn't move any of my furniture. The bed, desk, chair, and dresser are all still in the room.

M: That's odd. Well, did you move anything else from the room and put it in the hallway?

W: Uh . . . Oh, yeah. I remember. I took down those awful blinds from the window so that I could put up some curtains instead.

M: And did you, by chance, happen to place those blinds in the hallway after you took them down from the window?

W: Er . . . Yes, I did. Oh . . . I get it. That's the furniture I'm being accused of moving.

M: Yes, I believe that's correct. You see, you're not supposed to remove anything from the room without permission from this office.

W: Oh, sorry . . . So, uh, how do I get permission?

M: It's a fairly simple process. I can give you the form and approve it for you once you fill it out. However, we have to place the blinds into storage. The school has a place where you can put them although you're going to have to pay for them to be kept there. The standard fee for storing blinds for the entire semester is $100.

W: What? You mean I'm going to have to pay a total of $200 just so the school can put my blinds in some storage area for the whole year? That's utterly ridiculous.

M: Actually, you have to pay that amount as well as an additional $50 fine for removing furniture from your room without permission. I'm terribly sorry, but that's a school rule, and you violated it.

W: I can't believe this. Okay, whatever. Do I need to pay everything now, or can I pay it later?

M: Paying now is fine. Or if you prefer to wait, it will go on your bill, which you'll have to pay before the semester ends.

W: I'll take care of everything now so that I don't have to worry about this later on. Let me get my credit card from my purse.

Answer Explanations

1 Gist-Purpose Question

ⓓ At the start of the conversation, the student remarks, "Excuse me, but I found this notice here attached to the door of my dorm room today. According to it, I'm supposed to report to the student housing office at once."

2 Understanding Attitude Question

ⓑ The student says, "Look, um, can you tell me what's going on? I have a class to attend fifteen minutes from now, and it's practically on the other side of campus. I don't have much time to stay here." She is also very unhappy about having to pay a storage fee and a fine. By listening to the tone of her voice, you can tell that she is displeased with the man.

3 Detail Question

ⓒ The student declares, "I took down those awful blinds from the window so that I could put up some curtains instead."

4 Detail Question

2, 4 The student states, "You mean I'm going to have to pay a total of $200 just so the school can put my blinds in some storage area for the whole year?" Then, the man adds, "Actually, you have to pay that amount as well as an additional $50 fine for removing furniture from your room without permission."

5 Making Inferences Question

ⓐ After being told how much money she has to pay, the student announces, "I can't believe this." She is clearly shocked about how much money she has to pay.

PART 1 Lecture #1
p. 32

Script

Listen to part of a lecture in an economics class.

M Professor: Following Christopher Columbus's discovery of the New World in 1492, Spain began sending large numbers of expeditions westward across the Atlantic Ocean. Most went to Central and South America, where the Spanish proceeded to establish colonies that provided them with an enormous amount of wealth. 🎧10 Those riches allowed Spain to create a large trade-based empire, so it suddenly went from being a relatively modest land comprised primarily of farmers to the richest nation in Europe. Unfortunately for the Spanish, they squandered the majority of this wealth through mismanagement that resulted in high inflation and a decline in population. **Ultimately, the wealth did more harm to Spain than it did good.**

In the late fifteenth and early sixteenth centuries, Spain was mainly an agrarian nation with numerous peasant farmers as well as smaller classes of merchants, clergy, and nobility. It had a population of around, oh, ten million people or so, which was roughly the same number it had prior to the appearance of the Black Death in the mid-fourteenth century. The peasantry typically lived from hand to mouth and required good harvests to survive year after year. The merchant classes were based mainly in the coastal cities and in the great interior cities of Seville and Madrid. Much of the merchants' trade was based on wool textiles. As for the clergy, it would soon become powerful thanks to the Inquisition, which was a reaction to the growth of Protestantism in Europe. And last was the ruling class, which caused many of the problems that were to come in Spain.

Now, um, let's backtrack for a moment . . . As we discussed last week, Muslim conquerors had occupied large parts of Spain for centuries during the Middle Ages. The Spanish nobility expended a great deal of energy and bloodshed to defeat them and wound up expelling the last of the Muslim invaders in 1492. By that time, the members of the Spanish nobility had become highly militaristic and shunned any work that didn't befit their martial spirit. One result was that lots of talented men refused to become merchants or to work as government administrators. Instead, they idled their time on their vast estates while longing for military glory. This was one reason that so many of them sailed to the New World to become conquistadors: They were seeking wealth, fame, and military conquest. The attitudes of these men led Spain into a long period of warfare in the sixteenth century. This warfare pretty much wasted most of the newfound wealth coming in to Spain.

🎧 **11** The explorers who followed Christopher Columbus were looking for wealth, and they certainly found it in the New World. They obtained vast amounts of silver and gold there, and, each year, it was loaded onto ships and carried to Spain in a special treasure convoy. **Despite the best efforts of pirates and Spain's enemies, most of the wealth carried by these ships made it to Spain intact.** The influx of so much hard currency on an annual basis caused inflation not only throughout Spain but also in the rest of Europe. The Spanish spent a great deal of this wealth on luxuries and on expanding their military, and they subsequently got involved in prolonged wars with their neighbors, particularly the French and English.

As Spain increased the size of its overseas empire, its merchant class grew tremendously. With nearly all of the merchants based in port cities, wealth poured into Spanish coastal regions. Shipbuilding grew as did the textile industry. Seville nearly tripled in size during the sixteenth century and became a textile center. This led to the growth of the wool industry. Wool, of course, comes from sheep, and sheep must be raised in places with plenty of land and grass. The wealthy Spaniards involved in this industry began taking over peasant farming lands while flouting the

laws regarding the permitting of sheep to graze on farmland. Their actions resulted in a tremendous amount of land no longer being farmed, which severely affected the peasants. What happened next was a disaster. During the sixteenth century, there were several years of crop failures as well as a series of plagues, so Spain's population went into a severe decline. These problems also led to large numbers of beggars populating Spain's major cities as starving farmers sought work and then resorted to begging when none was to be found. Ah, and don't forget about the problems of inflation . . . Prices for many of the most basic goods increased by up to five times their original prices.

Basically, despite its large foreign empire, Spain suffered a series of disasters in the sixteenth century. It lost most of its wars . . . It spent most of its money . . . The supply of money coming from the New World decreased over time . . . And much of its peasant class either starved or was turned into beggars. In the end, by the year 1600, Spain's population declined from ten million to around 7.5, and its economy was in much worse shape than it had been when Columbus first sailed across the Atlantic.

Answer Explanations

6 **Gist-Content Question**

Ⓑ The professor spends most of the lecture telling the students about how the American colonies of Spain affected the country.

7 **Understanding Organization Question**

Ⓐ The professor tells the class, "By that time, the members of the Spanish nobility had become highly militaristic and shunned any work that didn't befit their martial spirit. One result was that lots of talented men refused to become merchants or to work as government administrators. Instead, they idled their time on their vast estates while longing for military glory. This was one reason that so many of them sailed to the New World to become conquistadors: They were seeking wealth, fame, and military conquest. The attitudes of these men led Spain into a long period of warfare in the sixteenth century. This warfare pretty much wasted most of the newfound wealth coming in to Spain."

8 **Detail Question**

③, ④ First, the professor declares, "During the sixteenth century, there were several years of crop failures as well as a series of plagues, so Spain's population went into a severe decline." Then, he adds, "Spain suffered a series of disasters in the sixteenth century. It lost most of its wars."

9 Making Inferences Question

Ⓑ The professor points out all of the negative results that happened to Spain due to its American colonies. As a result, he implies that Spain would have been better off if the country had not founded any colonies in America at all.

10 Understanding Function Question

Ⓓ When the professor mentions that the wealth did more harm than good to Spain, he is telling the students that the money Spain got caused problems instead of solving them.

11 Understanding Function Question

Ⓐ When the professor says, "Despite the best efforts of pirates and Spain's enemies," while talking about the special treasure convoys, he is implying that the convoys were often attacked while they were at sea.

PART 1 Lecture #2   p. 35

Script

Listen to part of a lecture in an environmental science class.

W Professor: Life in many of the Earth's ecosystems is so delicately balanced that, when one species encounters serious trouble, then there's often something of a, well, a domino effect on the other organisms in the ecosystem. To give you an in-depth look at what I'm talking about, let me turn your attention to one of the more unique ecosystems in the world. It's found in the high Arctic, and, uh . . . Let me get a picture of it here on the screen for you . . . Ah, yes, there it is . . . What you're looking at is a map of Franz Joseph Land, an archipelago in the Arctic Ocean north of the Russian mainland. There are 192 islands in the archipelago, which was discovered by an Austro-Hungarian expedition in 1873 and has been a part of Russia ever since 1926.

There are numerous land-dwelling and sea-dwelling animals residing on the islands and in the surrounding waters. The four major species that live on or near the islands are the polar bear, the walrus, the little auk, which is a species of bird, and the bowhead whale. In addition, in the water, there are seals, a wide variety of fish, and a great number of whelks, cockles, shrimp, sea urchins, and sea worms. There are also copepods. Those are a type of zooplankton that constitutes a major part of the biomass of the high Arctic Ocean. They're like tiny crustaceans, and they are one of the keystone species in the Arctic Ocean. Yes?

M Student: A keystone species? I'm sorry, but I'm not familiar with that term. Could you explain it, please?

W: Of course. Very simply, a keystone species is one that's a crucial part of its ecosystem. Without it, the ecosystem in which it resides may collapse. Think of the keystone in an arch. If you removed the keystone, the entire arch would fall down. That's how important a keystone species is. Well, in Franz Joseph Land, the copepods live mainly under the icecaps that cover most of the islands and descend into the surrounding waters. In the water under the icecaps grows a special type of algae which the copepods feed on. In turn, the huge colonies of little auks that live on the islands feed on the copepods. Oh, in case you're curious what it looks like, here's a picture of the little auk for you . . . This little bird lives on the islands in the Arctic Ocean in numbers so vast that zoologists estimate up to forty million of them may exist. 🎧17 Each summer season, little auks go to the islands to nest and mate in pairs on the steep cliffs found on most of the islands' shores. **As a side note for those of you interested in geology, these cliffs are products of the unique geography of the islands.** They were produced by a tectonic uplift that formed large columns of basalt stone, which made the islands primarily steep sided and flat topped.

So let me recap a bit. The islands have steep cliffs ideal for nesting sites . . . There are icecaps reaching into the water that produce algae, which attract copepods . . . And there's a perfect place for little auks. They thrive on copepods yet must eat thousands of the tiny creatures each day. And, yes, the copepods live in the water, but the wings of the little auk have evolved to let it both fly and swim, so feeding isn't a problem . . . as long as there's a food source. And here's where the primary problem lies. In recent years, the icecaps around the islands have grown smaller. This, in turn, has reduced the amount of ice over the water . . . which has reduced the growth of algae . . . which has additionally reduced the number of copepods in the area. So there's the potential for a crisis. If the copepods start disappearing, then the little auks will begin to disappear as well.

Scientists have been tagging little auks for years to track their movements to determine if the growing problem in the region will force them to move away to find new nesting grounds. But they're noticing that the instincts of the little auks appear to be causing them to return to the islands to nest and breed every summer. If the icecaps continue to get smaller, it's likely that the lack of food will cause the little auks to die in great numbers since they won't have a viable food source.

Keep in mind that it's not just the little auks that are being affected. Fish and whales also rely upon the copepods for food. Seals and walruses eat those fish, and, in turn, polar bears eat those seals and walruses. In fact, the huge colonies of walruses on the islands and seals living in the nearby waters are major sources of food for the polar bears. But the numbers of seals and walruses are declining so much that in recent years, some scientists have reported seeing polar bears eating grass and grazing as if they were cows. It appears that the entire ecosystem of the islands could be in serious danger, and that's something worrisome which needs to be closely monitored in the future.

Answer Explanations

12 Gist-Purpose Question

Ⓒ The student asks what a keystone species is, so the professor explains what it is.

13 Detail Question

Ⓐ The professor tells the students, "And here's where the primary problem lies. In recent years, the icecaps around the islands have grown smaller."

14 Connecting Content Question

②, ③ The professor states, "In recent years, the icecaps around the islands have grown smaller. This, in turn, has reduced the amount of ice over the water . . . which has reduced the growth of algae . . . which has additionally reduced the number of copepods in the area. So there's the potential for a crisis. If the copepods start disappearing, then the little auks will begin to disappear as well." Therefore, if the ice in Franz Joseph Land expands, it is likely that there will be more copepods in the area and that more animals will have their main food supply increased.

15 Making Inferences Question

Ⓐ The professor lectures, "In fact, the huge colonies of walruses on the islands and seals living in the nearby waters are major sources of food for the polar bears. But the numbers of seals and walruses are declining so much that in recent years, some scientists have reported seeing polar bears eating grass and grazing as if they were cows." She therefore implies that polar bears are catching fewer seals and walruses these days since their numbers are declining.

16 Understanding Organization Question

Ⓒ In the lecture, the professor first mentions the problem, and then she discusses what some possible results of the problem are.

17 Understanding Function Question

Ⓓ When the professor says, "As a side note," she is implying that what she is about to say is not relevant to the rest of the lecture.

PART 2 Conversation

p. 38

Script

Listen to part of a conversation between a student and a professor.

W1 Student: Professor Sturgis, you're having office hours right now, aren't you? Would you mind if I came in and spoke with you for a moment, please?

W2 Professor: Ah, hello. Actually, I don't have office hours today. I have them both tomorrow and on Friday; however, please feel free to come in. I don't have any classes or meetings today, so I have time to talk with you.

W1: Thank you, ma'am.

W2: Um . . . I really hate to admit this, but I'm afraid I don't recognize you. Do you happen to be enrolled in one of my classes?

W1: Yes, I am. My name is Dana Harper, and I'm a student in your Economics 101 class, uh, you know, Introduction to Microeconomics.

W2: Ah, that explains why I didn't recognize you. As you know, that class has more than 200 students in it. I'm really sorry, but I only get to know the names of a few students in a class that big. So . . . what can I help you with, Dana?

W1: Well . . . It's about my midterm exam. You see, I thought I had done a pretty good job on the test, but . . . when I got the exam back, I was totally shocked. I got a 74 on the test, and I'm not exactly sure why. I studied for a couple of days and thought I knew everything.

W2: Do you happen to have the exam with you? If I could take a look at it, then I could probably explain to you why you lost points on some of your answers.

W1: ⋒⁵Er . . . Sorry, but I left my test in my dorm room. **I guess, um . . . I guess I could run back to my dorm and get it if you want.**

W2: No, you don't need to do that since I've got to get going in a few minutes. However, before I leave, do you mind if I ask you a few questions?

W1: Questions? Sure.

W2: Okay . . . Let's see . . . What kind of notes do you take in my class? And where do you usually sit?

W1: I always sit in the back. Since it's an early morning class, I usually get to the classroom right as you're starting your lecture. I don't want to disturb anyone else, so that's why I sit in the back. As for notes . . . Well, uh . . . I don't bother taking any. Instead, I listen carefully to your lecture and then do all of the reading assignments listed on the syllabus.

W2: Hmm . . . You know, what you just told me might explain why you did poorly on the exam.

W1: What do you mean?

W2: First of all, it's nearly impossible for anyone to remember everything I say during my lectures. And you should be aware that a lot of what I teach is not covered in the textbook. So if you're mostly focusing on the textbook, you're missing out on a great deal of information. I suggest that you immediately start taking notes in the remaining classes. By doing that, you'll probably be able to improve your grade. In addition . . .

W1: Yes?

W2: Try to get to class earlier so that you don't have to sit in the back. It's a big auditorium, and it's difficult for students sitting so far away from me to hear me speak. I think you'll find that by sitting closer to the front, you'll hear me better and be able to pay closer attention in class.

Answer Explanations

1 Gist-Purpose Question

(D) When the professor asks the student how she can be of assistance, the student responds, "It's about my midterm exam. You see, I thought I had done a pretty good job on the test, but . . . when I got the exam back, I was totally shocked. I got a 74 on the test, and I'm not exactly sure why. I studied for a couple of days and thought I knew everything."

2 Detail Question

(B) When apologizing to the student, the professor remarks, "Ah, that explains why I didn't recognize you. As you know, that class has more than 200 students in it. I'm really sorry, but I only get to know the names of a few students in a class that big."

3 Understanding Attitude Question

(B) Regarding her grade, the student comments, "I was totally shocked. I got a 74 on the test, and I'm not exactly sure why."

4 Detail Question

[2], [3] First, the professor advises, "I suggest that you

immediately start taking notes in the remaining classes. By doing that, you'll probably be able to improve your grade." Then, the professor says, "Try to get to class earlier so that you don't have to sit in the back. It's a big auditorium, and it's difficult for students sitting so far away from me to hear me speak. I think you'll find that by sitting closer to the front, you'll hear me better and be able to pay closer attention in class."

5 Understanding Function Question

(A) When the student suggests going back to her dorm room, getting the test, and then returning with it, she is implying that she believes the professor will be in her office for a while.

PART 2 Lecture

p. 41

Script

Listen to part of a lecture in an anthropology class.

M Professor: The Americas, uh, you know, both North and South America, were one of the last places on the entire planet to be populated with humans. There's a theory that's pretty much accepted by most people regarding how the first humans came to the Americas. I'm sure you're all familiar with it. Basically, at the end of the last ice age sometime between 12,000 and 15,000 years ago, small groups of nomadic people crossed a land bridge across the Bering Strait between the lands that are modern-day Russia and Alaska. After these first people crossed into North America, nearly all of both North and South America were inhabited within, hmm . . . a thousand years or so. Interestingly, this theory may not be accurate. You see, um, we are finding evidence that people may have been in the Americas as many as 24,000 years in the past, and some of them may have arrived by sea rather than by walking across a land bridge.

In the past few years, we've been discovering bits and pieces of evidence that make it hard to reach a definite conclusion regarding when and how the first people came to the Americas. For one, we're not exactly sure what effect the various ice ages that happened in the past had on sea levels. That's important because, um, when ice ages took place in the past, they resulted in the sea levels in the north dropping. During some instances, the decline was enough to form a land passage, uh, a land bridge, across the Bering Strait. However, when the bridge developed, how many times it existed, and when people crossed it is hard to say.

As I just noted, there's some evidence that a small group of people came to the Americas 24,000 years ago. This evidence was found in a place in the Yukon region of Northern Canada in a place called Old Crow Basin. Animal bones unearthed in the region show some evidence of having been worked on by humans. What type of evidence, you may be wondering . . . ? Well, it includes the chipping of bones, which is typically caused by sharp objects. The same type of chipping is often found on animals killed by stone-tipped spears and worked on by stone knives. So, um, these bones were carbon-dated to 24,000 years ago. If humans did that, then there were people in the Americas 10,000 years earlier than what's commonly believed.

W Student: Couldn't the markings on the bones have been caused by something else?

M: Sure. That's possible. And that's the main argument people have against this evidence. They say the markings could have been made by rocks or by ice that moved after the animals died. So far, the evidence regarding a possible Yukon settlement is inconclusive.

W: Have any settlements been found in that region?

M: No, there haven't. And that's something else which people cite as proof that the bones were not chipped by humans. Thus far, no early settlements in that region or south of it have been found. Of course, there may have been no settlements in Old Crow Basin. Or perhaps the people who moved there were prevented from moving further south by ice sheets. Or, um, perhaps the small group retreated to Russia. Or maybe they died in the Yukon, and we simply haven't found their bones yet. As you can see, there are a lot of unknowns involved here.

W: So what is the earliest confirmed site we know about? Isn't that the Clovis people or something like that?

M: That's correct. The first strong evidence of an early settlement in the Americas comes from the Clovis site. In 1932, an important site was discovered in Clovis, New Mexico. Spear points used to kill mammoths were excavated there. Spear points made in the same style have been found at other places in the Americas, which suggests that the people who used them had a common point of origin. We've dated the Clovis site to roughly 11,500 years ago.

However . . . a site found in South America may actually be older. Artifacts and bones unearthed at a site in Monte Verde, Chile, have been dated to 12,500 years ago. That's 1,000 years before the Clovis site is dated. Do you see the problem . . . ?

W: 🎧11 Yeah, Chile is much further south than New Mexico. If people came from Russia, they would have had to journey all the way down through North America to get to Chile.

That could have taken centuries, so we should be able to find some really old sites elsewhere on the two continents.

M: That's pretty much what I had intended to say. And that's why some anthropologists, um, myself included, believe the Monte Verde settlers arrived by sea. Humans have been using boats for at least the past 40,000 years, so it's possible that people sailed across the Atlantic or Pacific Ocean and made it to the Americas. They most likely would have hugged the coastline as they sailed up and down the North and South American coasts. The most likely reason we haven't found any of their settlements yet is that they're underwater. Here, let me show you something . . .

Answer Explanations

6 Gist-Content Question

ⓒ The professor mainly lectures on how accurate the theory about how people first arrived in the Americas is.

7 Understanding Organization Question

Ⓐ The professor talks about the land bridge across the Bering Strait to discuss how people in ancient times have long been believed to have arrived in the Americas.

8 Detail Question

Ⓑ The professor lectures, "This evidence was found in a place in the Yukon region of Northern Canada in a place called Old Crow Basin. Animal bones unearthed in the region show some evidence of having been worked on by humans. What type of evidence, you may be wondering . . . ? Well, it includes the chipping of bones, which is typically caused by sharp objects."

9 Understanding Attitude Question

ⓒ The professor states, "And that's why some anthropologists, um, myself included, believe the Monte Verde settlers arrived by sea."

10 Understanding Organization Question

ⓒ The professor discusses a number of sites in the lecture and tells the students about what was found in them.

11 Understanding Attitude Question

Ⓐ When the professor responds to the student's comments by saying, "That's pretty much what I had intended to say," he is indicating his agreement with the student.

Actual Test 03

ANSWERS

PART 1

1 Ⓓ   2 Ⓑ   3 Fact: ③, ④   Not a Fact: ①, ②
4 Ⓓ   5 Ⓐ   6 Ⓑ   7 Ⓐ   8 Ⓒ
9 Erosion: ②, ③   Glacial Action: ①, ④
10 Ⓐ   11 Ⓒ

PART 2

1 Ⓓ   2 Ⓑ   3 Ⓑ   4 Ⓓ   5 Ⓐ
6 Ⓒ   7 Ⓐ   8 ②, ③   9 Ⓓ   10 Ⓓ
11 Ⓓ   12 Ⓑ   13 Ⓐ
14 Fact: ②, ③   Not a Fact: ①, ④
15 Ⓓ   16 Ⓐ   17 Ⓑ

PART 1 Conversation

p. 47

Script

Listen to part of a conversation between a student and a professor.

W Professor: Good morning, Martin. It's good to see you're out of the hospital. Are you feeling better these days?

M Student: Good morning, Professor Anderson. Uh . . . How did you know I was in the hospital? I thought only my friends and family members were aware of where I was.

W: The dean spoke with me. I imagine that one of your parents contacted the school to inform the administration about what happened. When a student suffers a major accident like you did, the administration alerts the dean of students, who then tells all of the student's professors so that we know what's going on. That way, when a student suddenly disappears from class for a couple of weeks, we don't think the student is merely skipping class.

M: Ah, I wasn't aware of that. That seems like a good policy for the school to have. Anyway, uh, to answer your question, yes, my condition has improved in the past few days. I'm still, uh, having trouble walking around a bit, but at least I'm not stuck lying in a hospital bed anymore. I'll need to be on crutches for at least the next three weeks though.

W: I sure hope you get better quickly.

M: Thanks for saying that. I appreciate it.

W: May I assume you're here to discuss what you missed during the past two weeks?

M: Yes, ma'am. That's correct. I, uh, I know I missed an exam last week. What am I supposed to do to make that up?

W: That's a good question. You'll have to take a makeup exam. According to school policy, you should take the exam within one week of returning to class.

M: One week?

W: Yeah, it's a pretty short time, isn't it?

M: You can say that again.

W: However . . . I prefer to be more lenient with my students, especially the ones I know are busy like you are, so I'll give you two weeks to take the test. How does that sound?

M: That would be great. That should give me enough time to learn the material I missed.

W: All right. So let's plan on you taking the test two weeks from today at . . . hmm . . . How does this time work for you?

M: It's fine. I don't have class right now. Should I visit your office to take the test?

W: Yes, you can take it in my office while I get some work done. Now, uh, what about notes? Do you have any friends in the class whose notes you can borrow?

M: 🎧5 Well . . . I have one friend in the class, but he doesn't take particularly good notes. I don't think that borrowing his notes would be beneficial to me at all.

W: In that case, I'll ask Emily Jackson if you can copy her notes. You'll be more than pleased to get a look at the notes she takes. I'll talk to her after tomorrow's class ends.

M: Excellent. Now, uh, one more thing. I believe you assigned a paper for us to write last week. Is that correct?

W: It sure is. You need to write a paper roughly eight to ten pages long. I gave the class a handout on it, so, uh, let me find a copy of it to give to you. Hold on just a moment while I figure out where I put those papers.

Answer Explanations

1 **Gist-Content Question**

Ⓓ The student and professor spend most of the conversation talking about the makeup work the student needs to do after he had an accident and missed class.

2 Detail Question

(B) When the student asks the professor how she found out about his injuries, she responds by saying, "The dean spoke with me. I imagine that one of your parents contacted the school to inform the administration about what happened. When a student suffers a major accident like you did, the administration alerts the dean of students, who then tells all of the student's professors so that we know what's going on."

3 Detail Question

Fact: 3, 4 Not a Fact: 1, 2

During the conversation, regarding the test, the professor says, "Yes, you can take it in my office while I get some work done." The student and professor also indicate that the material he missed will be on the test. However, it is not true that the students took the exam two weeks ago; they took the exam last week. And the student will have two weeks, not one, to prepare for the test.

4 Making Inferences Question

(D) At the end of the conversation, the professor states, "I gave the class a handout on it, so, uh, let me find a copy of it to give to you. Hold on just a moment while I figure out where I put those papers."

5 Understanding Function Question

(A) When the professor tells the student she will have Emily Jackson let him borrow her notes, she is implying that Emily Jackson takes excellent notes.

PART 1 Lecture

p. 50

Script

Listen to part of a lecture in a geology class.

M Professor: If there are no more questions about Monday's lecture, we've got a number of things to cover today, so why don't we get started with class . . . ? All right. We need to continue where we left off on Monday and keep discussing various land formations. The first one we have to explore is the gorge. Interestingly, this word comes from the French language and means either throat or neck. I think you'll understand why we use the word when I tell you what a gorge is. You see, uh, a gorge is a valley that has very steep sides—just like a throat has steep sides, right? In addition, gorges are usually found in rocky terrain and almost always have a river or stream at the bottom. There are three ways they form, and I'd like to cover them in depth now.

The most common way gorges form is through erosion. Basically, a river or stream flows across a region of hard, rocky land, and, over a period of thousands or even tens of thousands of years, the flowing water gradually erodes the upper layers of hard rock. Because the rock is hard, a wide, gentle valley doesn't form. Instead, a steep-sided, rocky gorge is created. In many of these types of gorges, the water erodes through layers of soft rock that's surrounded by regions of harder rock. Limestone, for example, is a common soft rock that erodes and forms steep-sided gorges. As the water flows, the sediment that's eroded is carried downstream, often to a large body of water, such as a lake, sea, or ocean. For example, the Colorado River, which formed the Grand Canyon, flows all the way to the Gulf of California. Now, uh, the depth of the gorge depends upon many factors. Basically, the bottom of the gorge, which is where the river or stream is located, is usually the same level as the large body of water that it flows into. So that's a determining factor regarding how deep the gorge is. Next, uh . . . Yes? Do you have a question, Sarah?

W Student: Yes, sir, I do. Regarding your statement about the depth of a gorge. What if it's a gorge that's forming? What will its depth be like then?

M: In that case, the water wouldn't be at the level of the large body of water it empties into. For that kind of gorge, you might have a combination of a shallow gorge with waterfalls somewhere along the way to the large body of water. Still, over time, the waterfalls will erode the rocks they flow over. As that happens, a gorge will form in a sort of backward manner. By that, I mean that it will retreat from the edge of the waterfall upstream. Oh, and there may also be a series of waterfalls when the river or stream flows from a high region of land to a lower one. In that case, the flowing water may form several gorges that eventually link up and become one long gorge after an extended period of time.

Okay, uh, how about the second way that gorges form . . . ? This happens through a combination of erosion and geological uplift. Sometimes the land rises through geological processes happening deep underground. This is typically caused by the rise of molten rock, which sometimes hardens as it cools. While the molten rock is moving upward, it pushes the land above it up, too. When this happens, low-lying land with water flowing through it can be raised high above the surrounding area. Then, the water will begin eroding the land to form a gorge in the newly raised higher region. Two examples of geological uplifting are the Colorado River and the Snake River, both of which are in the United States. Gorges in uplifted regions of land commonly have waterfalls, especially in places bordering the land that didn't get uplifted.

The third way a gorge can form is through glacial action. As large glaciers move through land, they cut deep notches in rocky terrain. If there's a region of very soft rock surrounded by harder rock formations, then a glacier may create a steep-sided gorge. During the last major ice age, this happened all over the northern regions of the world. When the glaciers retreated as the ice age ended, they left behind many steep-side gorges, and melted glacier water then simultaneously formed rivers in their bottoms. The Columbia River Gorge in Oregon is an example of a gorge formed through glacial action.

Just to give you an idea regarding the depths of gorges, let me show you some pictures. Look up here on the screen, please. Here's the Grand Canyon, which is a very wide gorge . . . Ah, yeah . . . you should know that canyon and gorge are pretty much interchangeable terms. Anyway, um, the Grand Canyon is about 1,600 meters deep yet isn't the world's deepest gorge. There's actually a debate on what the world's deepest gorge is since some experts use the depth from the highest point of the surrounding walls while others use a width-to-depth ratio. By using the width-to-depth ratio, the deepest and steepest gorge is the Vikos Gorge in Greece. Here's a picture of it . . .

Answer Explanations

6 Gist-Content Question

Ⓑ The professor spends most of the lecture discussing three different ways that gorges can be created.

7 Understanding Organization Question

Ⓐ About limestone, the professor remarks, "Limestone, for example, is a common soft rock that erodes and forms steep-sided gorges."

8 Detail Question

Ⓒ The professor points out, "Gorges in uplifted regions of land commonly have waterfalls, especially in places bordering the land that didn't get uplifted."

9 Connecting Content Question

Erosion: ②, ③   Glacial Action: ①, ④

Regarding erosion, the professor states, "Basically, a river or stream flows across a region of hard, rocky land, and, over a period of thousands or even tens of thousands of years, the flowing water gradually erodes the upper layers of hard rock." He then adds, "Now, uh, the depth of the gorge depends upon many factors. Basically, the bottom of the gorge, which is where the river or stream is located, is usually the same level as the large body of water that it flows into." As for glacial

action, the professor states, "The Columbia River Gorge in Oregon is an example of a gorge formed through glacial action." He also mentions, "When the glaciers retreated as the ice age ended, they left behind many steep-side gorges, and melted glacier water then simultaneously formed rivers in their bottoms."

10 Understanding Function Question

Ⓐ When telling the students to look at the screen, the professor says, "Look up here on the screen, please. Here's the Grand Canyon, which is a very wide gorge."

11 Understanding Organization Question

Ⓒ During his lecture, the professor explains in detail the three different ways that gorges are created.

PART 2 Conversation

p. 53

Script

Listen to part of a conversation between a student and a guidance counselor.

W Guidance Counselor: Hello. Please step into my office . . . May I assume you are David Jenkins?

M Student: Yes, ma'am. That's correct.

W: David, when I called you on the telephone to set up this meeting yesterday, you seemed a bit reluctant to come here to speak with me. Are you all right chatting with me for a few minutes today?

M: Uh . . . I guess. But, um, I'm kind of confused about why I'm here and why you even contacted me in the first place. Do you think you could tell me what this is all about?

W: I sure can, David. You see, a couple of your professors—uh, I'm not allowed to tell you their names—but, um, two of them reported that you seem somewhat stressed out these days.

M: Um . . .

W: Please let me finish if you don't mind.

M: Of course. Go ahead, please.

W: According to your professors, the quality of your work has drastically declined in the past month. They both commented that you appear to be dealing with a great deal of stress, but, when they asked you about it, you were unwilling to respond. These two professors were so concerned about your well-being that they contacted me, so that's why I got in touch with you.

M: I see.

W: 🎧4So . . . Is there something in your life going on that you'd care to discuss, David? You can feel free to speak with me. **Everything you say is strictly confidential and will be kept between you and me.**

M: Well . . . To be honest, this has been a pretty rough semester. I've had a few personal issues . . . uh, mostly family related . . . that have affected me, so I guess that's why the quality of my work has suffered.

W: Have these, er, family issues been resolved yet, or are they an ongoing matter?

M: 🎧5Hmm . . . For the most part, they're not an issue anymore. The main problem I presently have is that I'm so far behind in all of my classes that it's going to be hard to catch up with everything. And that's causing me a good deal of stress at the moment. **I mean, um, I'm studying practically every waking moment, but I don't know how I'm going to avoid getting poor grades in several classes this semester.**

W: Admitting you have a problem is the first step toward solving it. Now, um, may I suggest not focusing on your schoolwork all the time?

M: Huh? Why not?

W: Simple. If you do that, you'll get burned out. But don't misunderstand because I'm not telling you to quit studying. You need to keep studying, especially if you want to do well in your classes, yet you should be sure to take at least an hour a day to do something relaxing. You know . . . play a sport, hang out with your friends, or do something similar.

M: Okay. I can do those things. But what about my classes?

W: You need to tell me a few more details about your issues, and then I can have a chat with your professors. I won't tell them what the problem is—confidentiality, remember—but I will advise them to give you extra time to do your work. So are you ready to open up and talk to me?

M: If you can assist me like that, sure, I guess I can tell you everything that has been going on.

Answer Explanations

1 Gist-Purpose Question

Ⓓ The guidance counselor tells the student, "You see, a couple of your professors—uh, I'm not allowed to tell you their names—but, um, two of them reported that you seem somewhat stressed out these days."

2 Detail Question

Ⓑ The guidance counselor recommends, "You should be sure to take at least an hour a day to do something relaxing. You know . . . play a sport, hang out with your friends, or do something similar."

3 Making Inferences Question

Ⓑ At the end of the conversation, the student comments, "If you can assist me like that, sure, I guess I can tell you everything that has been going on." So he is probably going to continue speaking with the guidance counselor.

4 Understanding Attitude Question

Ⓓ When the guidance counselor states that everything the student says will be "strictly confidential," she means that she will not talk about their conversation with anyone else.

5 Understanding Function Question

Ⓐ The student points out that he is studying a lot yet is unlikely to get good grades. So he is implying that studying very much is probably not going to help him.

PART 2 Lecture #1 p. 56

p. 56

Script

Listen to part of a lecture in a history class.

M Professor: With that having been said, we have arrived at the end of the semester. We've got a few minutes left though, so, before I dismiss you, let me review a couple of things. I think it's absolutely crucial to your understanding of the Byzantine Empire that I emphasize its legacy. It's also something that's going to be on the final exam, so I suggest you listen closely, especially, um, if you didn't take many notes during the course of this semester. Recall that the Muslim Ottoman Turks finally managed to conquer Constantinople on May 29, 1453, and that victory signified the end of the Byzantine Empire, which had lasted for more than a millennium and was itself a remnant of the old Roman Empire.

Taking a look back at the Byzantine Empire, you should be able to see that without it, history for both Europe and the world as a whole would have been enormously different. Recall that while the Western Roman Empire collapsed during the late fifth century, the Eastern Roman Empire remained intact and in fact evolved into the Byzantine Empire. It served as a shield for the rest of Europe by protecting the Europeans from societies from the east that were constantly attempting to expand westward. For a time, of course, the Byzantines attempted to reconquer the land of the Western Roman Empire, which had fallen under the sway of invading barbarians, but they ultimately failed to do so.

While the Byzantines were not successful in that endeavor, in time, their failure actually proved to be a key turning point in the history of Western Europe. The reason is that the legacy of these invading barbarians was the successor states that we presently know as France, Italy, Germany, Spain, and England. Once the Byzantines realized they would not be able to retake the western lands, they concentrated on defending their own empire in the east. Soon afterward, a new threat emerged from the desert sands of Arabia: Islam. During the late seventh century, Muslim armies swept out of Arabia and went across the Middle East. In a rapid period of time, Muslim invaders conquered North Africa and sailed across the Mediterranean Sea. They invaded Spain and got as far as France before being stopped in the west by the Franks under Charles Martel at the highly pivotal Battle of Tours in 732. That marked the time when Muslim advances in Western Europe came to an end.

Meanwhile, in the east, the Byzantines and Muslims fought for centuries. Their wars were interrupted by periods of peace, but war was a constant fact of life. While the Byzantines remained an active bulwark against Muslim progress westward, Western Europe developed the modern states we're familiar with. The Byzantine Empire additionally served as a base for the Crusaders as they moved east to attempt to retake the Holy Land from the Muslims. Of course, the Crusaders eventually failed, and so did the Byzantine Empire. Its people and lands were gradually conquered so that, by 1453, only Constantinople was left, and, when it was finally taken, the empire vanished from history.

What happened prior to the fall of Constantinople served as another vital aspect of the Byzantine Empire's legacy. Preserved in Constantinople for centuries were numerous books and manuscripts from ancient Greece and Rome. 🎧11 With the end of the empire in sight, many people, including scholars, fled to the west and brought large numbers of those written works with them. The knowledge they preserved included ancient texts about art, mathematics, history, engineering, and architecture. **This rediscovered information played a key role in the onset of the Renaissance, which, incidentally, you can learn about next semester should you opt to take another course with me.**

Another unintended consequence of the defeat of the Byzantine Empire was that Europeans began searching for new trade routes. For centuries, trade from India and China had moved westward through Byzantine lands. But once the old routes were controlled by Muslims, Western Europeans were forced to find new ones. Some Europeans began sailing down the coast of Africa, whereupon they eventually arrived in the Indian Ocean and made their way to India. Other intrepid explorers sailed west across the Atlantic. Christopher Columbus discovered the Americas, and he was soon followed by other sailors such as John Cabot, Jacques Cartier, and Henry Hudson.

Those three points are essentially the legacy of the Byzantine Empire. Remember . . . The Byzantines served as a shield for Western Europe, they preserved a tremendous amount of knowledge from the ancient world, and the empire's collapse resulted in the discovery of new trade routes and entirely new lands. Of course, the third wasn't really the Byzantines' doing, yet it's still of consequence. You will be tested on these things on your final exam, which, incidentally, is scheduled for December 19 from nine AM to noon. You need to be in this classroom by nine. If there are no questions, then I believe we're done for the day . . . and the semester. Ah, yes . . . You?

Answer Explanations

6 Gist-Content Question

Ⓒ The professor spends most of the lecture discussing the legacy of the Byzantine Empire.

7 Understanding Organization Question

Ⓐ About the Battle of Tours, the professor remarks, "In a rapid period of time, Muslim invaders conquered North Africa and sailed across the Mediterranean Sea. They invaded Spain and got as far as France before being stopped in the west by the Franks under Charles Martel at the extremely pivotal Battle of Tours in 732. That marked the time when Muslim advances in Western Europe came to an end." Thus she stresses the historical importance of the battle.

8 Detail Question

2, 3 First, the professor states, "It served as a shield for the rest of Europe by protecting the Europeans from societies from the east that were constantly attempting to expand westward." Then, he comments, "Preserved in Constantinople for centuries were numerous books and manuscripts from ancient Greece and Rome. With the end of the empire in sight, many people, including scholars, fled to the west and brought large numbers of those written works with them. The knowledge they preserved included ancient texts about art, mathematics, history, engineering, and architecture. This rediscovered information played a key role in the onset of the Renaissance."

9 Detail Question

Ⓓ The professor mentions, "Another unintended consequence of the defeat of the Byzantine Empire was that Europeans began searching for new trade routes."

10 Making Inferences Question

Ⓓ At the end of his lecture, the professor tells the class, "If there are no questions, then I believe we're done for the day . . . and the semester. Ah, yes . . . You?" Since he calls on a student, he will probably answer that individual's question next.

11 Understanding Attitude Question

Ⓓ When the professor says, "This rediscovered information played a key role in the onset of the Renaissance, which, incidentally, you can learn about next semester should you opt to take another course with me," he is implying to the students that he is going to teach a class on the Renaissance in the next semester.

PART 2 Lecture #2

p. 59

Script

Listen to part of a lecture in a zoology class.

M Professor: We don't have much time left, so I'd like to discuss one more animal in brief. It's the badger, which is one of nature's great diggers. Take a look up here on the screen . . . Ah, there it is. There are eleven species of badgers. Most live in Europe although the honey badger resides in Africa and parts of Asia while the American badger can be found in America. There are a few minor differences between species, but most share some common characteristics. For example . . . A badger's body is short and squat while its neck is elongated. Some species can grow up to nearly one meter in length. A badger's ears are small, and its head typically has white and dark fur, um, sometimes in striped patterns whereas its body tends to be grayish in color. The badger is an omnivore, so it eats plants as well as animals, and it has sharp teeth and strong jaws. The badger's best-known features are its short, powerful legs and its long, sharp claws, which it uses to dig its home.

The badger lives underground in a burrow called a sett. That's spelled S-E-T-T. A sett can be comprised of a few tunnels and rooms with one or two entrances, or it can be an elaborate complex with more than ten entrances, dozens of rooms, and numerous tunnels connecting everything.

The badger usually prefers to live in dry ground that's easy to shift. In America, for instance, most badgers reside in prairies. In a sett, there may only be a single badger, but what's more usual is a family of them. While up to fifteen badgers have been found living in a single sett, six are much more common. A badger keeps its sett very clean and tolerates no garbage in it. It brings in grass, straw, leaves, and other plant matter for bedding as it lines its main chambers with these materials to sleep more comfortably. But when spring comes, the badger removes the vegetation and brings in new material throughout the summer to prepare for the coming winter. The badger does not urinate or defecate in its home either. Instead, it digs a shallow pit away from the sett to use as a latrine. In fact, the badger is so clean that it won't even bring any food into its home.

All right, so what about the badger's diet? Well, it varies from species to species, but most of them love insects, worms, grubs, and small invertebrates. It also eats snakes and lizards as well as the occasional bird, and it has been known to attack hedgehogs and rabbits. The badger sometimes eats berries and fruit, and it digs up the roots of some plants to eat as well. It's a nocturnal animal, so it hunts at night and rests during the day, so . . . Um, yes? Do you have a question for me?

W Student: What about the honey badger? Does it only eat honey?

M: No, it doesn't. 🎧17 The honey badger got its name because of its love of honey. However, it eats a wide range of other foods, including, um, snakes, lizards, birds, and bird eggs. **As a general rule, badgers are not very fussy when it comes to food.** Some, such as the honey badger, have special tastes, but most will eat whatever is available. You should also be aware that the badger is relentless in its pursuit of food. It will go after animals sheltering underground by using its large claws to dig up the ground, and then it will pin its prey down and devour it. The badger doesn't leave much behind either as it consumes the skin, bones, and most other parts of whatever it catches. Nor is it timid. It attacks venomous snakes, including the deadly cobra, and even hunts turtles since its powerful jaws can crack the hardest of turtle shells. Some naturalists in Africa have actually observed badgers chasing away adult lions and taking their recent kill. Basically, the badger is not an animal you want to mess with.

Okay, um, let me say a few words about the mating habits of the badger really quickly. Male badgers are boars while female badgers are sows. Sows can mate when they're about two years old, and when they pair up with a boar, the two remain together for life. The badger has something of an unusual reproductive cycle. Depending upon the species, its mating season may be in the spring, summer, or fall. Yet the fertilized eggs don't implant themselves in the sow's uterus until December. After that, there's a seven-week gestation period. A sow produces a litter of between one and five young. After being born, the young stay in the sett for up to two months. They're quite helpless as they're blind for the first month of their lives, and they depend upon their mother's milk for four or five months. Okay, um, that's all we have time for today. But before you leave, let me tell you about your homework.

Answer Explanations

12 Detail Question

(B) About the badger's appearance, the professor remarks, "A badger's body is short and squat while its neck is elongated. Some species can grow up to nearly one meter in length. A badger's ears are small, and its head typically has white and dark fur, um, sometimes in striped patterns whereas its body tends to be grayish in color."

13 Making Inferences Question

(A) The professor implies that the badger will attack animals more dangerous than it when he comments, "Nor is it timid. It attacks venomous snakes, including the deadly cobra, and even hunts turtles since its powerful jaws can crack the hardest of turtle shells. Some naturalists in Africa have actually observed badgers chasing away adult lions and taking their recent kill. Basically, the badger is not an animal you want to mess with."

14 Detail Question

Fact: 2, 3   Not a Fact: 1, 4

About the sett, the professor points out, "A sett can be comprised of a few tunnels and rooms with one or two entrances, or it can be an elaborate complex with more than ten entrances, dozens of rooms, and numerous tunnels connecting everything." The professor further notes, "A badger keeps its sett very clean and tolerates no garbage in it. It brings in grass, straw, leaves, and other plant matter for bedding as it lines its main chambers with these materials to sleep more comfortably. But when spring comes, the badger removes the vegetation and brings in new material throughout the summer to prepare for the coming winter. The badger does not urinate or defecate in its home either. Instead, it digs a shallow pit away from the sett to use as a latrine. In fact, the badger is so clean that it

won't even bring any food into its home." The professor does not say that the badger has a room in its sett for a latrine. Instead, it digs a pit away from the sett. And up to fifteen badgers, not twenty, may live in a single sett.

15 Understanding Organization Question

(D) During the lecture, the professor provides the students with many facts about the characteristics of the badger.

16 Making Inferences Question

(A) At the end of the lecture, the professor tells the students, "But before you leave, let me tell you about your homework."

17 Understanding Attitude Question

(B) When the professor says that badgers "are not very fussy when it comes to food," he means that they will eat virtually anything.

Actual Test 04

ANSWERS

PART 1

1 Ⓑ	2 Ⓓ	3 ①, ④	4 Ⓓ	5 Ⓐ
6 Ⓐ	7 Ⓐ	8 Ⓓ	9 Ⓐ	10 Ⓐ
11 Ⓒ	12 Ⓐ	13 Ⓑ	14 Ⓓ	15 Ⓓ
16 Ⓐ	17 ①, ③			

PART 2

1 Ⓒ	2 ③, ④	3 Ⓐ	4 Ⓑ	5 Ⓑ
6 ①, ③	7 Ⓒ	8 Ⓓ	9 Ⓑ	10 Ⓑ
11 Ⓒ				

PART 1 Conversation

p. 65

Script

Listen to part of a conversation between a student and a History Department office secretary.

W1 History Department Office Secretary: Good afternoon. Welcome to the History Department office. Is there something I can help you with today?

W2 Student: Hello. I'm looking for Mrs. Cynthia Goodman. Do you happen to know if she's here today?

W1: Actually, that's me. What do you need me for, young lady?

W2: Oh, hi. It's nice to meet you, Mrs. Goodman. My advisor, uh, Professor Wright, told me there's a job opening here for a student assistant this semester. He said I ought to come here and speak with you about it. He also mentioned that he was planning to talk to you about me. Er . . . Did he happen to do that?

W1: Not exactly. Professor Wright commented that I should expect a student of his to inquire about the position, but he didn't give me your name. He was kind of in a hurry when he spoke with me this morning, so giving me that bit of information must have slipped his mind.

W2: Oh . . . I see.

W1: Anyway, you're here, and I know he's the one who sent you. That's the important part. Shall I tell you about the job?

W2: Yes, ma'am. I would appreciate that. What would you need me to do?

W1: You'd be working directly for me, so you'd pretty much just be doing basic office work.

W2: Such as . . . ?

W1: You know, you'll have to do some typing . . . some filing . . . and copying. Lots and lots of copying. You're going to become really familiar with the copy machine if you take this job. Professors are always requesting copies of papers in order to give handouts to their students.

W2: That seems perfectly all right to me. I usually work at my father's company during the summer, and I do similar types of jobs there.

W1: Oh, that's interesting. Are you a good typist?

W2: I type around eighty words per minute. So I guess I'm faster than most people, but I've also had tons of practice.

W1: That's an impressive number. You type faster than most of the secretaries at the school do. I'll definitely have you do a great deal of typing . . . uh, assuming you take the job, that is.

W2: Is there anything else I would do besides what you just mentioned?

W1: Hmm . . . You might have to run errands every once in a while. For instance, you might need to visit another department to pick something up. Most student employees like doing that type of thing since it gives them a chance to get out of the office.

W2: Yeah, that makes sense to me. What are the hours like?

W1: I'd prefer if you worked at least twelve hours a week. You can decide which days you will work, but it would be ideal for you to work four hours a day three days a week. I don't want you working fewer than three hours a day though.

W2: Okay, that sounds possible. In fact, I've got a good amount of empty space in my schedule this semester, so I think I could manage to work four days a week.

W1: That sounds great. Can you show me when you're thinking of working each day?

W2: Yes, I can do that. I've got a copy of my schedule right here.

Answer Explanations

1 Understanding Function Question

Ⓑ About Professor Wright, the student remarks, "My advisor, uh, Professor Wright, told me there's a job opening here for a student assistant this semester. He said I ought to come here and speak with you about it."

2 Understanding Attitude Question

Ⓓ After the secretary explains the job duties, the student declares, "That seems perfectly all right to me. I usually work at my father's company during the summer, and I do similar types of jobs there."

3 Detail Question

1, 4 First, the secretary notes, "You know, you'll have to do some typing . . . some filing." Then, she mentions, "You might have to run errands every once in a while. For instance, you might need to visit another department to pick something up."

4 Detail Question

Ⓓ The secretary states, "It would be ideal for you to work four hours a day three days a week."

5 Making Inferences Question

Ⓐ The student is fine with the job duties and says that she can work the hours that the secretary would like, so it can be inferred that she will accept the job if it is offered to her.

PART 1 Lecture #1 p. 68

Script

Listen to part of a lecture in an astronomy class.

M Professor: When I was young, I saw the movie *Close Encounters of the Third Kind*. It came out in the 1970s, so I doubt many of you have seen it. Anyway, it's about the first human contact with an alien race. As I watched the movie, I was really looking forward to my first glimpse of the aliens on that spaceship. When they appeared, they were bipeds and were humanlike with arms, legs, a head, and eyes. That's something which is very common in science fiction, uh, both in movies and literature: It's the notion that alien life will look somewhat human. But is that the reality of what's waiting for us somewhere out there . . . ?
Will organisms, uh, you know, extraterrestrial life in the rest of the universe resemble those that live on the Earth . . . ?

All right, uh, for the purpose of this lecture, let's assume that the Earth is not the only place in the universe with life on it. Personally, that's my belief although I'm sure several, um, or even many, of you believe differently. But keep in mind that there are literally billions of other planets in the Milky Way Galaxy alone. We've discovered thousands of them already, and some appear to be rather Earthlike. With so many worlds out there, the chances that some of them could support life of some form or another is extremely high. In my opinion, sometime during my lifetime, we will receive proof that we aren't alone but that alien life actually exists.

What will these aliens look like . . . ? That's a good question. It's highly possible that life on another planet will not conform to the same principles that it does on Earth. There are, however, some basic factors that simply cannot be ignored. For instance, various conditions that kill life on our planet may not be fatal in other places. For instance, the lack of gases such as oxygen or the absence of water may not prohibit life from existing. When it comes to alien life, we need to think outside the box and dispose of any preconceived notions of where life will live, what it will look like, and how it will act. After all, even here on the Earth, there are organisms that can survive in extreme conditions. Let me see . . . Life exists in frigid Antarctica and in incredibly hot volcanoes, and certain organisms can survive in extremely acidic, salty, or radioactive environments that would kill humans who tried living in them. Why wouldn't aliens be able to do the same thing?

In my opinion, since life can exist in those types of conditions on the Earth, it should be able to do so on other planets as well. That means we need to accept that not all life on other planets will be oxygen-breathing, meat-and-plant-eating, humanlike or animal-like lifeforms. In all likelihood, when we find the first evidence of extraterrestrial life, it will be incredibly simplistic. My guess is that the majority of life existing elsewhere is microbial in nature. Why is that . . . ? Well, we already know that microbes can survive in harsh environments. Take, for example, the microbes in a cave in Mexico that get their energy through chemical interactions with sulfur as well as the microbes found at the bottom of a lake deep beneath the Antarctic ice cap. Those microbes can survive extremes of cold and pressure as well as low levels of light and oxygen, all conditions which are very harsh. Microbes are extremely adaptable, so that makes them strong candidates for being the predominant lifeforms elsewhere.

But I don't want to focus on what tiny alien life may look like. That's not particularly interesting. Instead, I'd like to think about larger, uh, multi-celled organisms and intelligent alien life in particular. First of all, we need to consider that the planet or moon any alien life develops and evolves on will have a tremendous effect on what the creatures look like. For instance, consider a planet that has mostly water on its surface. Any advanced life forms on it may resemble something akin to the fish populating our seas since it will have adapted to survive in its environment. And here's an interesting thought . . . Consider a planet with gravity stronger than that of the Earth. Organisms that evolve in a high-gravity environment almost assuredly won't be bipeds like us. The simple explanation is that two legs won't be strong enough to support the creatures' bodies in gravity that's so high. Instead, alien life on that planet would likely have short, squat bodies. It could have multiple legs as well to help it move more easily.

Those are just a couple of thoughts on what aliens might look like. Right now, let me show you a bunch of pictures. These are images of how some astronomers and xenobiologists believe aliens might appear depending upon their home environments. Let's get started. Here's an image of what aliens that evolved on a gas giant might look like . . .

Answer Explanations

6 Gist-Content Question

Ⓐ The primary topic of the lecture is how extraterrestrial life will appear.

7 Understanding Attitude Question

Ⓐ The professor tells the students, "In my opinion, sometime during my lifetime, we will receive proof that we aren't alone but that alien life actually exists."

8 Making Inferences Question

Ⓓ The professor comments, "For instance, the lack of gases such as oxygen or the absence of water may not prohibit life from existing." Then, he mentions, "That means we need to accept that not all life on other planets will be oxygen-breathing, meat-and-plant-eating, humanlike or animal-like lifeforms." He therefore implies that alien life may be able to breathe gases other than oxygen.

9 Detail Question

Ⓐ The professor declares, "Microbes are extremely adaptable, so that makes them strong candidates for being the predominant lifeforms elsewhere."

10 Understanding Function Question

Ⓐ The professor states, "Consider a planet with gravity stronger than that of the Earth. Organisms that evolve in a high-gravity environment almost assuredly won't be bipeds like us. The simple explanation is that two legs won't be strong enough to support the creatures' bodies in gravity that's so high."

11 Connecting Content Question

Ⓒ The professor points out that the environments of the planets will determine what aliens look like, so it can be inferred that aliens that live on gas giants and those that live on watery worlds will look different from one another.

PART 1 Lecture #2

p. 71

Script

Listen to part of a lecture in a history class.

W Professor: If you have ever visited the countryside in England, one of the things you must have noticed was the ubiquity of hedges that divided fields and gave certain regions a checkerboard-like appearance. Oh, um, for those of you who aren't aware, a hedge is a row of plants growing together very closely and forming a barrier which looks like a wall of sorts. In England, the most common plants used to make hedges are the hawthorn, blackthorn, and holly.

I'd like to talk a bit about hedges to let you know the role they played in the history of England. Landowners have used hedges to divide and enclose their lands since the time when there were Romans living in England. This tradition continued though the Anglo-Saxon Period and into the Middle Ages. However, it wasn't until the great expansion of farmland which happened between the thirteenth and fifteenth centuries that hedges became so widespread. As landowners cleared their land of trees so that they could plant crops, they began planting hedges on the boundaries of their property. They did this for three main reasons. First, it was aesthetically pleasing to have neat, orderly boundaries . . . Second, it helped landowners know where their land ended and their neighbors' began . . . And third, it helped stop other people from using their land.

In the past, virtually anyone could use land in England. People in a region had traditional rights permitting them to use the common land, or commons, as it was often called. They would cut hay for their livestock and allow their animals to graze on these common grounds. This open field system additionally made it difficult for landowners to know if their neighbors were planting crops on their own land or other people's lands. So, uh, looking at it from the landowners' point of view, you can see why they wanted to grow hedges and to have their fields enclosed. After all, the hedges clearly marked boundaries and prevented other people's animals from grazing on land that didn't belong to them. Hedges also stopped other people from planting crops on property that wasn't theirs.

Meanwhile, the common people in England, as you can imagine, felt differently than the landowners. They believed the growing of hedges infringed on their rights and traditions. They suffered a great deal when wealthy landowners started asserting control over common lands by planting hedges and enclosing fields. The common people couldn't feed their animals as much as they had in the past, nor could they grow as much food. They protested the planting of hedges. At times, these protests grew so heated that blood was shed and lives were lost.

While the rate at which hedges were planted increased after the thirteenth century, it wasn't that fast. But the situation changed in the eighteenth and nineteenth centuries. During that period, there was a massive enclosure movement across the entire country.

M Student: What caused that change? The only thing I can think of which happened during that time was the Industrial Revolution, but that couldn't account for the enclosure movement, could it?

W: Well, you're both right and wrong, Greg. The enclosure movement actually was a direct result of the Industrial Revolution. You see, uh, the first industry affected by the Industrial Revolution in a major way was the textile industry. The invention of the steam engine enabled laborers using looms in factories to make textiles at unprecedented rates. Of course, they needed huge amounts of raw materials to make those textiles. Does anyone know what that raw material was? Greg . . . ?

M: Hmm . . . Wool maybe? Oh . . . Now I get it.

W: All right, class, it appears as though Greg has just worked everything out. Well done, Greg. The primary raw material used in the textile industry back then was indeed wool, which comes from sheep. Sheep need grass to feed on, and that created a demand for enclosed grazing lands. Wealthy people in England began buying land all around the country and promptly planted hedges around their property to close off the land. That kept the sheep in and people out. Here's an interesting fact for you: Hedges became so popular that an entire new industry arose as some individuals started growing hawthorn, blackthorn, and other hedge plants to sell to wealthy landowners.

The enclosure movement had a tremendous effect on England. Since more land was used for grazing, less land was used for farming. This led to a rise in unemployment in the countryside since fewer people were able to find work on farms. Many of these suddenly jobless individuals protested, which resulted in riots and bloodshed. That led to Parliament passing laws defending the rights of landowners to do whatever they pleased with their land. Remember that wool was directly responsible for creating an unprecedented amount of wealth in England at that time, so the government was protecting the people raising the sheep. As for those who lost their jobs, well, many had no choice but to move to the growing cities to seek work in factories. While many people have vilified the landowners for their actions, personally, I don't see it that way. Let me explain to you why . . .

Script

Listen to part of a conversation between a student and a professor.

W Professor: Larry, is there something I can help you with? I was just about to go home for the day.

M Student: Oh . . . In that case, would you rather that I come back at a later time? I guess I could return here tomorrow in the afternoon.

W: Well, you're already here, and I don't have anything particularly urgent to do, so why don't you come on in and have a seat?

M: Thanks for saying that, ma'am. I appreciate it.

W: Okay, so what would you like to discuss?

M: I intend to write a senior thesis next year, and I'd like for you to be my advisor on the project.

W: That sounds possible, but first I need to ask you a few questions . . . To begin with, do you realize how much work is going to be involved in writing a senior thesis? It's a two-semester obligation, and it's going to occupy a huge amount of your time.

M: Yes, ma'am. I've spoken with a couple of seniors who are presently writing them, and they've both let me know that I need to be completely dedicated to the project to do a good job on it. That's why I've decided not to play on the school's soccer team in the fall like I normally do.

W: Okay. Are you planning on doing an internship or working part time next year?

M: I'm definitely not doing an internship, so there's no need to worry about that. And, uh, yes, I have a part-time job, but it's in the engineering library. So, uh, it doesn't get many students. I basically sit at the front desk and check out books every once in a while. But when I'm not busy, I can do my homework, so it's not like my job there is taking away from my school time.

W: Hmm . . . That's a good job you've got there.

M: Yes, ma'am, I rather like it.

W: All right. It appears as though you won't have any major obstacles in finding enough time to do the research for the project. That's refreshing. All too often, students try taking on way too many tasks their senior year, and they wind up having to drop them, or they do poorly on them. I hope that doesn't happen to you, Larry.

M: I'll make sure to do my best to avoid any negative consequences, ma'am.

W: Now, finally . . . Have you thought of a topic you'd like to write about for your thesis?

M: Er . . . That is sort of why I'm here. Obviously, I'd like to do something regarding ancient Greek history since that's the focus of my major, but, uh . . .

W: You don't know what to do yet, right?

M: Yeah, exactly. I mean, uh, a senior thesis is supposed to be some kind of original scholarship, right?

W: That's correct. Students should do research on a topic that hasn't been explored before.

M: Well, um . . . I'm not sure what I could do that no one has ever researched. Do you happen to have any ideas?

W: Not off the top of my head, but I can give you the titles of some books to read that might be able to help us come up with something. Come back here tomorrow morning, and I'll give you a list of, uh, five or six books. When you finish reading them, we can meet here, discuss the books, and then think of a topic that you can write about.

M: Awesome. Thanks so much, Professor Neff.

Answer Explanations

1 Gist-Content Question

Ⓒ At the beginning of the conversation, the student says, "I intend to write a senior thesis next year, and I'd like for you to be my advisor on the project." Then, the student and the professor spend the majority of the conversation discussing that.

2 Detail Question

③, ④ Regarding his activities next year, first, the student notes, "That's why I've decided not to play on the school's soccer team in the fall like I normally do." Then, he comments, "And, uh, yes, I have a part-time job, but it's in the engineering library. So, uh, it doesn't get many students. I basically sit at the front desk and check out books every once in a while. But when I'm not busy, I can do my homework, so it's not like my job there is taking away from my school time."

3 Understanding Function Question

Ⓐ The professor asks, "To begin with, do you realize how much work is going to be involved in writing a senior thesis? It's a two-semester obligation, and it's going to occupy a huge amount of your time." She does that to find out if he will have a workload that is too heavy or not.

4 Detail Question

Ⓑ The professor tells the student, "I can give you the titles of some books to read that might be able to help us come up with something. Come back here tomorrow morning, and I'll give you a list of, uh, five or six books."

5 Making Inferences Question

Ⓑ The professor says, "Come back here tomorrow morning, and I'll give you a list of, uh, five or six books. When you finish reading them, we can meet here, discuss the books, and then think of a topic that you can write about." In saying that, she is implying to the student that she will serve as his thesis advisor.

PART 2 Lecture

p. 77

Script

Listen to part of a lecture in an environmental science class.

M Professor: In very cold places, lakes usually freeze over in the winter. Nevertheless, the fish living in these lakes still manage to survive this extreme change to their environment. When I was younger, I always wondered how they managed not to die, and I bet many of you are curious about this as well. Well, um, one reason they don't die is that they've evolved in a variety of ways to ensure their survival.

But another reason, about which I'd like to speak now, is that the entire lake does not freeze. Instead, only the top layers freeze whereas the water in most of the lake remains in its liquid form. Here's what happens . . . When the temperature starts decreasing in fall, the upper layers of the lake cool first. As the water cools, it becomes denser. When the water in the upper layer reaches a temperature of four degrees Celsius, it attains maximum density and sinks. As it sinks, warmer water beneath it rises to the surface to balance the volume. Then, this water cools and sinks, and more water rises.

This rising and falling of water helps delay the freezing of the lake for some time. This cycle continues until the water temperature in the entire lake gets to four degrees Celsius. When that happens—and it almost always does in the very cold regions of the Northern Hemisphere—then the water in the upper layers of the lake stops cycling and remains where it is. When the water temperature drops to zero degrees Celsius, the lake begins to freeze. Yet the cold never reaches the lower levels, so much of the lake stays liquid. Lake fish are cold blooded and have no way to warm themselves, so it's fortunate for them that the temperature in the water remains above freezing. Nevertheless, it's

quite cold, so the fish adapt mainly by slowing down their movements. They become lethargic and seem almost to be hibernating like many mammals and reptiles do. The fish usually descend to the bottom of the lake, where it's the warmest since it's far from the frozen upper layers. They also tend to hide from running water in places such as behind rocks or in deep pools, so that prevents them from moving much.

🎧**11** Because the fish are so inactive, their metabolisms slow down as well, which benefits them since food is typically scarce in cold water. Small fish are the primary food source for large fish, so the smallest ones don't normally survive very cold winters, especially since other food sources, such as insects, aren't present during the winter months. **Still, since the metabolisms of fish slow down, food that would normally take them a day to digest in summer remains in their digestive systems for up to a week in the winter.**

Slowing down their bodies additionally helps fish conserve oxygen. The oxygen level in the water starts declining once the lake begins freezing. Fish extract oxygen from the water through their gills, but, when the top layer is frozen, the amount of oxygen getting into the lake is much less than it is in summer. Of course, there's some oxygen trapped in the water under the ice, but it decreases in amount as winter progresses. By being inactive and having metabolisms that are slowed down, fish can cope with the scanty amount of oxygen in the lake.

W Student: Professor Chambers, do all lake fish act in the same way when winter comes?

M: Not at all. There are many differences in how they act depending upon the species. Some lake fish are profoundly affected by the cold while others hardly notice any difference. Let's see . . . The trout is a very active fish all throughout the winter months. While most fish sit motionless at the bottom of a frozen lake, trout can be found much higher up—often just about two meters or so beneath the frozen ice. That's one reason ice fishermen commonly catch trout in winter. Trout also tend to expand their range of habitation in winter as they move to regions dominated by larger fish that go dormant during cold weather. The onset of winter is additionally good for fish such as walleye and northern pike. They eat much better when winter begins. The reason is that the water plants in which small fish frequently hide die as winter approaches, and this exposes the small fish, which then become meals for larger fish such as walleye and northern pike. By eating well and fattening up, the larger fish can ensure that they survive long winters.

On the other hand, bass move very slowly, become dormant

during winter, and eat only enough to ensure that they survive. Carp and catfish move little, too. They usually lie on the bottom . . . sometimes buried in mud . . . and seem virtually to sleep winter away. In case you wonder how we know this, many of these fish have been tagged with tracking devices by researchers. So they've been observed moving to a spot when winter begins and hardly moving from it until spring arrives.

Answer Explanations

6 Gist-Content Question

1, 3 During his lecture, the professor talks mostly about the reactions of various species of fish when the water gets cooler and the manner in which lakes partially freeze.

7 Detail Question

C The professor notes, "This cycle continues until the water temperature in the entire lake gets to four degrees Celsius. When that happens—and it almost always does in the very cold regions of the Northern Hemisphere—then the water in the upper layers of the lake stops cycling and remains where it is."

8 Detail Question

D The professor points out, "Slowing down their bodies additionally helps fish conserve oxygen."

9 Understanding Organization Question

B The professor talks about how the trout increases its activity in winter when he says, "The trout is a very active fish all throughout the winter months. While most fish sit motionless at the bottom of a frozen lake, trout can be found much higher up—often just about two meters or so beneath the frozen ice. That's one reason ice fishermen commonly catch trout in winter. Trout also tend to expand their range of habitation in winter as they move to regions dominated by larger fish that go dormant during cold weather."

10 Connecting Content Question

B The professor talks about how the walleye and the bass have differing levels of activity during winter.

11 Understanding Function Question

C Since food that would get digested in one day in summer takes one week to be digested in winter, the professor implies that fish eat much less than normal during winter.

Actual Test 05

ANSWERS

PART 1

1 Ⓓ	2 Ⓐ	3 3, 4	4 Ⓒ	5 Ⓑ
6 1, 4	7 Ⓑ	8 Ⓑ	9 Ⓒ	10 Ⓐ
11 Ⓓ				

PART 2

1 Ⓓ	2 Ⓑ	3 Ⓐ	4 Ⓒ	5 Ⓐ
6 Ⓒ	7 Ⓑ	8 Ⓒ		

9 Camouflage: 4　　Species Recognition: 2, 3
Warning: 1

10 Ⓑ	11 Ⓐ	12 Ⓐ	13 Ⓑ	14 Ⓑ
15 Ⓓ	16 Ⓐ	17 Ⓒ		

PART 1 Conversation　　　　p. 83

Script

Listen to part of a conversation between a student and the dean of students.

W Student: Good morning, Dean Chandler. My name is Susan Jones. It's a pleasure to meet you. I really appreciate your taking some time out of your busy schedule to speak with me today.

M Dean of Students: The pleasure is all mine, Susan. Why don't you have a seat, and then you can tell me why you were so eager to schedule a meeting with me?

W: Thank you very much . . . So, uh, I'm a junior at this school, and I really love it here. But I have to admit that my freshmen year here was, uh, not so pleasant.

M: Is that so? Would you mind explaining why?

W: Not at all. Basically, I didn't have a clue as to what was going on my first year of college. I mean, uh, I wasn't sure what classes to take . . . I couldn't find a job on campus even though I really needed to work part time . . . and, uh, I didn't know much about any of the extracurricular activities which were available to me. In a word, I suffered from a lack of information.

M: I'm really sorry to hear that.

W: It was tough, but I worked hard to learn about the school and figured out what kinds of opportunities were available to me. And that's what I'm here to speak with you about today.

M: Okay.

W: I would like to set up a kind of information center on campus. It would be specifically aimed at first-year students. I want it to, uh, to assist students in integrating with the campus. It could provide information—and advice—on classes, social life, jobs, and various other topics.

M: You know, er, we already have organizations and people who do these kinds of activities here at the school. For example, professors provide advice to students regarding the classes they should take. You yourself have an advisor, right?

W: That's correct.

M: We also have a job placement office on campus, and then there's the student activity center that helps with extracurricular activities. Are you not aware of these things?

W: I am, and I have two points to make regarding them.

M: Go ahead.

W: First, they're run by regular employees, not students. So, uh, sure, these people can tell us about jobs and classes and activities, but they can't give us a student's perspective. My proposed information center would be staffed by students who could provide first-hand experience, which would be much more useful than the information students are getting nowadays.

M: What's your second point?

W: To be frank, most of the employees at these offices couldn't care less about their jobs. If you ask them about something, they usually just hand you a pamphlet. That's neither inspiring nor interesting.

M: Hmm . . . I'm a bit alarmed to hear you say that. I'll have to look into the matter. Now, uh, as for your idea, I'm intrigued. Can you write up a formal plan for it, including staffing and how much money you think you'll need?

W: Sure, I can do that for you. Is, um . . . how about submitting it to you by the beginning of next week?

M: That's perfect. Just drop it off with my secretary. I'll read over it and then contact you to set up an appointment to discuss the matter.

Answer Explanations

1 Gist-Content Question

Ⓓ The speakers mostly talk about the student's idea on how information about the school could be shared better.

2 Understanding Function Question

Ⓐ The student tells the dean of students about some of the hardships she had to endure during her first year of college when she says, "Basically, I didn't have a clue as to what was going on my first year of college. I mean, uh, I wasn't sure what classes to take . . . I couldn't find a job on campus even though I really needed to work part time . . . and, uh, I didn't know much about any of the extracurricular activities which were available to me. In a word, I suffered from a lack of information."

3 Detail Question

3, 4 The student says, "I want it to, uh, to assist students in integrating with the campus. It could provide information—and advice—on classes, social life, jobs, and various other topics."

4 Understanding Attitude Question

Ⓒ The student shows that she believes some of the employees on campus are not particularly interested in her jobs when she comments, "To be frank, most of the employees at these offices couldn't care less about their jobs. If you ask them about something, they usually just hand you a pamphlet. That's neither inspiring nor interesting."

5 Detail Question

Ⓑ The dean of students tells the student, "Can you write up a formal plan for it, including staffing and how much money you think you'll need?"

PART 1 Lecture p. 86

Script

Listen to part of a lecture in a zoology class.

W Professor: This creature you're looking at on the screen is one of the more common species of termite . . . Notice the typical white coloring as well as the body shape, which is similar to that of the ant. In fact, it's so similar that the termite is called the white ant in Australia. Like ants, termites live in colonies consisting of thousands—or even millions—of them. How many live in a single colony varies from species to species, and there are roughly 3,000 species of termites in the world, so there's a good amount of variation. Most termites reside in tropical and subtropical regions although a few live in temperate zones. Termites prefer the tropics since they need moisture to survive. Without it, their bodies will shrivel up and die. Naturally, this means that termites aren't found in arid places like deserts but instead frequently establish their colonies in damp, woody places, such as inside dead trees, or in huge mounds near a source of vegetation.

Being near vegetation is crucial for termites since they eat cellulose. That is, as I hope you know, the substance that comprises the cell walls of plants. Termites prefer wood since it has plenty of cellulose. In fact, they simply thrive on wood, which is why they're a danger to wooden structures. Let me talk about that more in just a bit though . . . I want to focus on their colonies right now. A termite colony is based on a rigid social structure in which there are both leaders and followers. In the termite world, the leaders are the adults which become the king and queen. Only a termite that grows wings can become a king or queen. Not all termites grow wings though, and, of those which do, only one becomes the king and another the queen in each colony. In some species, the winged termites which don't become the king or queen move away to establish colonies of their own. Now, uh, when the king or queen dies, another winged adult may take its place. The king and queen mate frequently and remain companions for their entire lives, which may be a decade or more. The queen also grows larger than her male companion to give birth in the form of eggs, of which she may lay tens of thousands at a time.

Once the queen lays her eggs, they're placed in what are called nursery chambers, and they soon hatch and produce larvae. The larvae undergo the nymph stage and then the adult stage through metamorphosis. As it goes through each stage, a termite's skin molts so that it can grow larger. Interestingly, not all termites achieve total adulthood, which, by the way, includes the development of wings. Instead, the vast majority simply become non-adult workers. Their duties include building the colony, finding food, storing food, taking care of the eggs, and raising the young. Worker termites typically have life spans of around two years.

Other non-adults may become soldiers, which defend the colony from intruders. In most species, the soldiers look slightly different from the workers. While they are still pale white in color and have similar body shapes, their mandibles—uh, their jaws—are larger and sharper. These mandibles enable soldier termites to attack enemies that might invade the colony. Ants sometimes attack termite colonies, and so do beetles, birds, toads, centipedes, and even some bears. Here's something that's interesting: Some species of termites don't have larger mandibles but instead have a different defense mechanism. They can spray a sticky, poisonous substance at their enemies. That's kind of cool, huh . . . ? Oh, and some termite species have no soldiers but instead rely upon worker termites and immature nymphs for protection.

M Student: Professor Stanton, a minute ago you said you were going to talk about what termites eat. Can you cover that now?

W: That's the next topic I intend to cover, Jose. So, uh, what about their diets? As I said earlier, termites love to eat cellulose. This makes any kind of vegetation—especially wood—their primary source of food. In some ways, this provides a number of benefits for the ecosystems termites live in. After all, termites break down dead plant matter, and their feces go directly into the soil, which helps rejuvenate it. Unfortunately, termites also cause problems for people. Uh, yes, Jose?

M: That's very true. A termite colony set up in my family's barn, and the termites wound up destroying a large part of it. It cost us a lot of money to get rid of them.

W: Yes, that happens sometimes, class. You see, when termites establish a colony inside a wooden structure, they'll eventually eat through most of the wood in the building and thereby cause severe structural damage to it. Fortunately, there are ways to prevent this from happening. For instance, people can frequently exam the structure, use pesticides to drive away or kill the termites, and keep the structure dry. That's a crucial one since termites won't found a colony unless a place is already damp.

Answer Explanations

6 **Gist-Content Question**

1, 4 The professor spends most of the lecture talking about which food termites consume as well as the duties that different types of termites have. Although she does talk about where termites prefer to build their mounds, that is not a major part of the lecture, so ⓒ is not a correct answer.

7 **Understanding Organization Question**

ⓑ The professor states, "Most termites reside in tropical and subtropical regions although a few live in temperate zones. Termites prefer the tropics since they need moisture to survive. Without it, their bodies will shrivel up and die."

8 **Detail Question**

ⓑ According to the professor, "A termite colony is based on a rigid social structure in which there are both leaders and followers. In the termite world, the leaders are the adults which become the king and queen." She also discusses the various chores that other termites have.

9 Connecting Content Question

Ⓒ The professor says, "Interestingly, not all termites achieve total adulthood, which, by the way, includes the development of wings." Thus when a termite becomes an adult, it will develop wings.

10 Detail Question

Ⓐ The professor declares, "In most species, the soldiers look slightly different from the workers. While they are still pale white in color and have similar body shapes, their mandibles—uh, their jaws—are larger and sharper."

11 Understanding Attitude Question

Ⓓ About termites, the professor mentions, "As I said earlier, termites love to eat cellulose. This makes any kind of vegetation—especially wood—their primary source of food. In some ways, this provides a number of benefits for the ecosystems termites live in. After all, termites break down dead plant matter, and their feces go directly into the soil, which helps rejuvenate it."

PART 2 Conversation

p. 89

Script

Listen to part of a conversation between a student and a professor.

M1 Professor: Hello, Jim. What brings you here to my office? I figured you'd be outside enjoying the nice spring weather today.

M2 Student: Good afternoon, sir. Um, I wish I could hang out with my friends. That would be nice, but since I was sick for the past two weeks, I've been busy making up a lot of the work that I missed. As a matter of fact, I finished doing the makeup lab for your class a couple of minutes ago.

M1: Ah, that's right. I had forgotten about that. Well, I'm glad to hear you're catching up with all of the work you need to do. It must be tough trying to get everything done since we're closing in on the end of the semester.

M2: It isn't easy. I can tell you that much. But I'm still doing my best.

M1: That's a good attitude to have, Jim. I'm sure you'll manage to complete your assignments on time. So, um, are you here to submit your lab report?

M2: On the contrary, I need to speak with you about the experiment I ran. I got some results that were, um . . . unexpected I guess is the word I ought to use.

M1: How so?

M2: Well . . . would you mind taking a look at this, please? These are the results I got when I conducted the experiment. Here you are . . .

M1: Hmm . . . These are rather odd . . .

M2: Yeah.

M1: Jim, are you sure you followed the instructions exactly as I gave them to you? If you ran the experiment properly, there's no way you would have gotten these results. They simply don't make any sense at all.

M2: I'm positive I didn't do anything wrong when I conducted the experiment, sir. I checked and double-checked to make sure I was doing everything properly. After all, I really have no desire to redo the experiment.

M1: 🎧⁵It looks like you may have to though.

M2: That's what I was afraid of. What do you think the problem could be?

M1: Well, in a case like this, human error is the most likely explanation.

M2: But . . .

M1: I know you're a good student, Jim. In fact, you're pretty much at the top of this class, but it's entirely possible that you made a mistake when you conducted the experiment.

M2: Yes, I suppose you're right. But, um . . . what if I didn't make a mistake? What do you think the problem could be?

M1: Hmm . . . My guess is that there's something wrong with the equipment. It's probably the laser that you used. Perhaps it needs to be recalibrated.

M2: Uh . . . How do I fix that problem? I've got no experience at repairing lasers, so I haven't a clue what to do.

M1: That's not a problem for you to handle, Jim, nor is it something I want you to attempt. That laser is an extremely expensive piece of equipment, so students aren't allowed to do anything out of the ordinary with it. Hmm . . . You know, I've got a couple of hours before I have to attend a faculty meeting. Why don't both of us go down to the lab and do the experiment together? That way, we can determine what went wrong. How does that sound?

M2: Great. I'm finished with my classes for the day, so I've got plenty of time. Thanks a lot for offering to help me out, sir.

Answer Explanations

1 Gist-Purpose Question

Ⓓ When the professor asks the student if he is there to submit his lab report, he responds, "On the contrary, I need to speak with you about the experiment I ran. I got some results that were, um . . . unexpected I guess is the word I ought to use."

2 Detail Question

Ⓑ The student mentions, "That would be nice, but since I was sick for the past two weeks, I've been busy making up a lot of the work that I missed."

3 Understanding Attitude Question

Ⓐ When the student comments that he needs to work hard to complete all of his assignments, the professor praises him for being willing to work hard.

4 Understanding Function Question

Ⓒ About the laser, the professor notes, "My guess is that there's something wrong with the equipment. It's probably the laser that you used. Perhaps it needs to be recalibrated." So he is stating that the laser could be the cause of the problem.

5 Understanding Function Question

Ⓐ When the professor comments, "Human error is the most likely explanation," he is indicating to the student that he probably made an error while he was conducting the experiment.

PART 2 Lecture #1 p. 92

Script

Listen to part of a lecture in a marine biology class.

W Professor: All of the colors of the rainbow—plus many others—can be seen under the surface of the ocean as every species of fish has its own distinct coloring and patterns. Why this is so is one of the unsolved mysteries of science. The problem we have is that we don't really understand how fish eyes work and how their brains interpret color. Another issue is that there are a wide variety of fish eyes, all of which have differences regarding their shapes, sizes, and even their alignments on the bodies of the fish. Compound those problems with the fact that the eyes of various species of fish have evolved differently based upon the lighting conditions and clarity of the water in which they live, and it's therefore difficult for marine biologists to know how fish see and understand colors in addition to knowing why fish have certain colors on their bodies. On top of all that, we tend to use our own perspectives when making judgments about such things. So, uh, while we may believe that a fish's color pattern acts as camouflage, it might, in fact, be that color for an entirely different purpose . . . Be that as it may, let me give you some possible reasons that fish are certain colors.

The first is a reason I just mentioned: camouflage. This is a real possibility because it simply makes sense in numerous cases. For instance, many species of fish are dark colored on the top and light colored on the bottom. Codfish and haddock are two such examples, uh, as are many species of sharks and dolphins. The most logical reason for this coloring is that the dark colors help the fish blend in with the dark regions beneath it when it's viewed from above. Likewise, when viewed from below, the light coloring on the bottom of its body helps the fish blend in with the sky and lighter regions above it. As a result, predators in the water— uh, other fish—and predators out of the water, such as birds, have difficulty seeing the fish.

Take a look at page, uh . . . page 294 in your books, please . . . That's a picture of a coral reef. Notice the fish in the picture . . . Their colors help them blend in with their ecosystem. ⚲11 Coral reef fish are frequently as brightly colored as the coral and marine plants inhabiting the reefs. The colors of these fish more easily enable them both to hide from predators and, uh, for the fish which are predators, to lie hidden while waiting for prey to swim by. **But let me remind you of one thing: Since we don't know how fish see these colors, while they appear to blend in with their surroundings to our eyes, the same may not be true for various species of fish.**

A second strong possibility for fish coloring is that fish have different colors so that others of their own kind can recognize them. Species recognition is important in the animal world since it lets them tell friend from foe and know the members of their own families. You see, uh, even within a species, individual animals often have different patterns and colors. Take a look at the poster on the wall over there to my right . . . See those two tropical fish . . . ? At first glance, their colorings look identical, right . . . ? But look more closely . . . There are some slight differences. What does that mean . . . ? Well, it's possible that these differences enable fish to recognize individual members of the same species—possibly for familial recognition or mating purposes. This could be extremely useful in places such as coral reefs, which are often crowded with huge numbers of fish. For instance, fish that can easily recognize others can save energy by avoiding having to take aggressive measures too often.

A third possibility is that colors act as warnings to other fish.

There are two ways this could work. Here's the first . . . Most poisonous fish are either brightly colored or have distinctive color patterns. The lionfish, for instance, has colorful stripes. These could act as a deterrent by indicating to other fish that they should stay away from it because the brightly colored fish is dangerous.

A second possibility is that fish warn others of their own species when danger is approaching. By experimenting with UV—uh, ultraviolet—light detection cameras, scientists have discovered that many species of fish can make and see colors in the UV range of the electromagnetic spectrum. Here's an example . . . The blue damsel fish, which lives in the South Pacific Ocean, sometimes flashes warnings to other fish in its school by using UV colors. It's believed that only other blue damsel fish can see this color burst. When flashed, the lights cause all the fish in the school to move sharply in a new direction. The fish does this when predators are approaching, so it's clear that this light is acting as some sort of a, uh, a warning beacon for other fish.

Answer Explanations

6 Gist-Content Question

ⓒ The professor spends most of the lecture discussing the purposes of the various colors fish have.

7 Detail Question

ⓑ The professor points out, "The problem we have is that we don't really understand how fish eyes work and how their brains interpret color."

8 Understanding Function Question

ⓒ During the lecture, the professor tells the students, "Take a look at page, uh . . . page 294 in your books, please . . . That's a picture of a coral reef. Notice the fish in the picture."

9 Connecting Content Question

Camouflage: 4   Species Recognition: 2, 3
Warning: 1
Regarding camouflage, the professor says, "Likewise, when viewed from below, the light coloring on the bottom of its body helps the fish blend in with the sky and lighter regions above it." As for species recognition, the professor remarks, "Well, it's possible that these differences enable fish to recognize individual members of the same species—possibly for familial recognition or mating purposes. This could be extremely useful in places such as coral reefs, which are often crowded with huge numbers of fish. For instance, fish that can

easily recognize others can save energy by avoiding having to take aggressive measures too often." And concerning warning, the professor lectures, "The lionfish, for instance, has colorful stripes. These could act as a deterrent by indicating to other fish that they should stay away from it because the brightly colored fish is dangerous."

10 Detail Question

ⓑ The professor states, "The blue damsel fish, which lives in the South Pacific Ocean, sometimes flashes warnings to other fish in its school by using UV colors."

11 Understanding Attitude Question

ⓐ When the professor declares, "While they appear to blend in with their surroundings to our eyes, the same may not be true for various species of fish," she means that while humans may not be able to see the fish, the fish might be visible to other fish.

PART 2 Lecture #2 p. 95

Script

Listen to part of a lecture in a history class.

M1 Professor: In the year 1909, American explorer Robert Peary reached the highest point on the planet, uh, the North Pole. That left only one major place on the planet that no human had ever visited: the South Pole. In the early twentieth century, several expeditions undertook the challenge, yet all of them failed. Then, in 1911, two teams—one Norwegian and the other British—both set out on a race to reach the South Pole. Ultimately, the Norwegian team triumphed. Led by the great polar explorer Roald Amundsen, the Norwegians reached the South Pole on December 14, 1911.

Despite Amundsen's achievement, when most people talk about this story, they focus on the failure of the British team and how its members met their deaths in the cold reaches of the Antarctic continent. And that's precisely what we're going to do now. The British team was led by Robert Falcon Scott, a naval officer who had previously visited Antarctica on an expedition from 1901 to 1904. Scott was clearly aware of the harsh conditions on the continent, which is why many historians, including myself, are puzzled as to why he made so many bad decisions both while preparing for the 1911 expedition and during the trek itself.

M2 Student: Could you give us an example of a mistake that he made, Professor Kirke?

M1: Sure. One of the more controversial decisions Scott

made concerned the choice of animals to help his team. It was well known then that teams of strong dogs, uh, such as huskies, were the best choice of animal for hauling sleds laden with supplies. Scott brought some of those dogs, but he also chose two other transportation methods: ponies and motorized vehicles. Unfortunately for him and his men, neither of those was suitable for the frigid conditions. You see, uh, ponies that could work well in cold weather were available, but the people responsible for procuring the animals for Scott had little experience with those animals, so they picked the wrong breed of pony. In addition, when the expedition arrived in Antarctica, the motorized vehicles proved to be virtually unworkable in the extreme cold. They frequently broke down, and one was so heavy that it broke through the ice and sank into the water.

Despite these setbacks, Scott's team pushed forward. Using the ponies, dogs, and motorized vehicles that worked, they began building forward supply bases. Then, Scott made another fateful decision . . . He decided to rely mainly on the ponies to establish a supply base at eighty degrees south latitude. He called this base One Ton Depot, and he intended for it to be the main supply base for the smaller team that was going to push on to the South Pole. It was also supposed to be a place that the returning team could easily reach and then resupply themselves before heading back to the primary expedition base. Unfortunately, the ponies selected weren't up to the task. Some died, and then, when they were almost fifty kilometers short of the goal, Scott decided that the ponies couldn't continue. He therefore established the One Ton Depot supply base short of where he wanted it. This decision ultimately cost him his life.

Here's another poor decision that affected the expedition's fate. Originally, four men were supposed to go to the South Pole, but Scott suddenly changed his mind and went with a five-man expedition. This meant that they needed more food, so they had to recalculate all the weight and transportation figures that had already been done for four men. Some historians argue that this didn't affect the fate of the expedition; however, I disagree with them. But it's definitely true that the decision not to use dogs or even ponies on the final trip to the South Pole was bad. The reason is that the men had to haul all of the supplied on sleds by themselves.

W Student: But wouldn't the dogs have died just like the ponies did?

M1: Probably not. Amundsen took dogs all the way to the South Pole and back. His team killed a few of the dogs for food, but many of the dogs proved tough enough to make

the trip. Amundsen started with around fifty dogs, and eleven survived the round trip. That's one reason people are so critical of Scott's decision to leave the dogs behind; they could have made a difference.

Anyway, on the final leg, the five British men were on their own. They reached the South Pole on January 17, 1912, a few weeks after the Norwegians had gotten there. Amundsen had left a flag and a tent at the South Pole, so Scott knew they had been beaten. On the return trip, the mistakes Scott had made wound up killing them. Weakened by a lack of food, extremely bad weather, and their physical efforts, the team halted about eighteen kilometers short of One Ton Depot. Too weak to continue and with no way to communicate with their main base, they died there in a tent. Scott's final diary entry was on March 29, 1912, but exactly when he died is uncertain.

12 Gist-Content Question

Ⓐ In his lecture, the professor mainly discusses the reasons that the expedition to the South Pole led by Robert Falcon Scott failed.

13 Understanding Attitude Question

Ⓑ About Scott, the professor states, "Scott was clearly aware of the harsh conditions on the continent, which is why many historians, including myself, are puzzled as to why he made so many bad decisions both while preparing for the 1911 expedition and during the trek itself."

14 Detail Question

Ⓑ The professor tells the students, "It was well known then that teams of strong dogs, uh, such as huskies, were the best choice of animal for hauling sleds laden with supplies."

15 Detail Question

Ⓓ The professor notes, "He therefore established the One Ton Depot supply base short of where he wanted it. This decision ultimately cost him his life."

16 Connecting Content Question

Ⓐ During the lecture, the professor mentions that Robert Falcon Scott used ponies and dogs whereas Roald Amundsen only took dogs to the South Pole.

17 Understanding Organization Question

Ⓒ The professor talks about the events that happened on Robert Falcon Scott's expedition to the South Pole in chronological order.

Actual Test 06

ANSWERS

PART 1

1 (A) 2 (B) 3 Fact: [2], [3] Not a Fact: [1], [4]
4 (D) 5 (C) 6 (B)
7 Fact: [2], [3] Not a Fact: [1], [4]
8 (A) 9 (B) 10 (A) 11 (C) 12 (C)
13 (A) 14 (B)
15 Hydrogen: [1], [2] Oxygen: [3], [4]
16 (B) 17 (D)

PART 2

1 (B) 2 (D) 3 (C) 4 [1], [3] 5 (B)
6 (C) 7 (B) 8 (D)
9 Fact: [1], [2], [4] Not a Fact: [3]
10 (A) 11 (D)

PART 1 Conversation

Script

Listen to part of a conversation between a student and a dining services employee.

W1 Student Dining Services Employee: Hello. My secretary mentioned that you'd like to speak with me about something regarding the dining halls. What can I do for you?

W2 Student: Uh, yes. My name's Stephanie Carter, and I'm a junior here at the school. It's nice to meet you, ma'am.

W1: It's nice to meet you as well, Stephanie.

W2: So, uh, my question is . . . What happened to all of the trays at the dining hall? I went to Lionel Hall to have lunch this afternoon, but, uh, when I got there, there weren't any trays for me to put my food on. It was really annoying trying to carry around a couple of plates, utensils, and a glass without dropping everything.

W1: Ah, yes, the trays. Well, we have a new policy here at the university's dining halls.

W2: A new policy? What? Like no trays?

W1: Yes, precisely. Starting this semester, we are no longer providing trays at any of the five dining halls we run on campus.

W2: Seriously?

W1: Yes, I'm very serious about that.

W2: Um . . . Why would you do that? Like I just said, carrying my lunch was extremely difficult. I nearly dropped everything on the floor. In fact, I saw one student drop her plate, and another student spilled his drink all over his pants because he was carrying too many things. So, uh, what reason could you possibly have for getting rid of the trays?

W1: This summer, every department at the school was instructed by the new president of the university that we need to find ways to reduce our usage of natural resources. This includes both electricity and water consumption. The only way we could do that at the dining halls was to get rid of the trays.

W2: How is that going to help anything?

W1: Without any trays, there will be fewer items to wash, so, as a result, we'll use much less water than we did in the past.

W2: ∩⁵Uh . . . Okay. But what are you going to do about all of the plates, bowls, and glasses that are going to break throughout the year when students drop them since they don't have any trays? I can't remember ever seeing anyone break something in my first two years here, but I saw that happen today, and it's only the first day of school. **I bet the money you spend replacing every broken item is going to be more than the money you save in electricity and water usage.**

W1: I see your point, but we didn't really have any choice due to the order made by the school president. Let me add that it won't do you any good to complain to me. I suggest that you make a complaint to her.

W2: Why would she listen to me?

W1: She might not listen to a single student, but, if a large group of students were to complain, perhaps we would be able to return things to normal at the dining halls.

W2: Ah, yes, I see your point. I'll try to get a few students to protest, and, uh, later in the week, I'll start a petition to return the trays to the dining services.

W1: I would greatly appreciate it if you did that. Personally speaking, I understand your argument and wish we could change things, but there's nothing I can do about it at this time.

Answer Explanations

1 Gist-Purpose Question

  (A) When the student goes to the man's office, she

Actual Test 06   35

asks, "What happened to all of the trays at the dining hall?"

2 Detail Question

ⓑ The student tells the woman, "In fact, I saw one student drop her plate, and another student spilled his drink all over his pants because he was carrying too many things."

3 Detail Question

Fact: ☑2☑, ☑3☑   Not a Fact: ☑1☑, ☑4☑

The student mentions, "I'll try to get a few students to protest, and, uh, later in the week, I'll start a petition to return the trays to the dining services." She does not, however, announce that she will make an appointment with the school president, and she says nothing about encouraging employees to go on strike.

4 Making Inferences Question

ⓓ The woman says, "She might not listen to a single student, but, if a large group of students were to complain, perhaps we would be able to return things to normal at the dining halls." Then, she adds, "I would greatly appreciate it if you did that. Personally speaking, I understand your argument and wish we could change things, but there's nothing I can do about it at this time." So it can be inferred that she disagrees with how the new president's policy is affecting the dining halls.

5 Understanding Function Question

ⓒ When the student makes that comment, she is indicating that she believes the school will lose money because of the new policy, so it will therefore be a waste of money.

PART 1 Lecture #1   p. 104

Script

Listen to part of a lecture in a botany class.

W Professor: One of the harshest environments on the entire planet can be found in the cold northern regions near the Arctic Circle. Largely located in northern Russia, Canada, Alaska, and Scandinavia, this land is called tundra. To survive in this environment, organisms have had to adapt in various ways. For the next few minutes, I'd like to focus on some of the plants that can be found growing in the planet's tundra regions.

But first, um, I think I ought to explain the conditions of the tundra region with regard to plant growth. As I just stated, tundra is a tremendously harsh environment. And as we know, plants require sunlight, warmth, a supply of water, and good soil to grow. Well, let's think for a moment . . . Water isn't much of a problem in the Arctic, but sunlight and warmth are definitely in short supply. The summer season only lasts about two months, and it's a cold summer there as temperatures rarely get higher than ten degrees Celsius. There is plenty of sunshine during the summer since the Arctic experiences almost continuous daylight during that time, but, again, that's true for just a few months. The rest of the year, the weather is brutally cold, there's often snow on the ground from September to June, and winter has almost perpetual darkness.

As for the soil, well, that's another problem since it's usually frozen for ten months of the year. And even when the soil thaws, it doesn't do so completely. About a meter beneath the surface, there's a layer of ground that's permanently frozen. It's called permafrost. Uh, I think you can figure out why it's called that, right . . . ? Because of permafrost, most Arctic plants have shallow root systems since they cannot grow very deep underground. Yet another issue in the Arctic is the wind. With no trees to block it, the wind is severe and tends to blow continuously. To adapt to this problem, most Arctic plants are short and squat, so they grow low to the ground, which enables them to avoid being ripped out of the soil by the wind. Furthermore, Arctic plants typically grow very close together, which provides them with added protection from the wind. They also frequently have hairy stems, which are hair-like growths covering their stems and providing them with added warmth.

🎧**11 Considering the cold temperatures, the low amount of sunlight for much of the year, the shallow soil, and the strong winds, it's practically a miracle that any plants live in the Arctic at all.** But they do, and botanists have identified almost 1,700 different species of plants living in the world's tundra regions. Most of them are lichens, mosses, shrubs, and grasses, but there are even some flowering plants that produce berries. Two special adaptations allow flowering plants to bloom. First, some of these plants begin sprouting even when there's still snow on the ground. That enables them quickly to produce flowers once the short summer growing season starts. In addition, these plants have short leaves, which permit them to retain water better since most plants lose water through their leaves.

Up here on the screen I'd like to show you some pictures of these tough Arctic plants. First off, we have Arctic moss . . . It's one of the most common plants in the tundra zone. It's often seen growing at the bottom of dried lake beds like this one . . . and around bogs, uh, like this . . . Arctic moss produces no flowers and reproduces by releasing spores into the wind. This plant serves a special purpose in the Arctic. It grows in thick carpets, which helps keep the land warmer, which, in turn, allows other plants to grow. All right, um, next is the Arctic willow . . . a small leafy green shrub that often covers vast areas of ground. Its green leaves turn red in late summer. See them here . . . The Arctic willow is a food source for animals such as caribou, musk oxen, and Arctic hares.

This plant here . . . is one of the more common berry-producing plants in the tundra: the bearberry. Note the short skinny leaves . . . the red berries . . . and the pale white flowers . . . The flowers can also be pink, like these here . . . The bearberry blooms between March and June and is one of the most commonly seen plants in the tundra during the summer months. Its red berries are a source of food for many birds inhabiting the region. Ah, and, of course, for bears, which is how the plant got its name. Up next is the diamond leaf willow . . . It produces slender leaves on branches that bend easily. This green plant forms in thick carpets and has fluffy white flowers some people think resemble caterpillars. The diamond leaf willow is highly prized by the Inuit people as its leaves are a rich source of vitamin C. They actually contain ten times as much vitamin C as an orange does, and their bendy branches are useful for making baskets as well. Okay, let's look at another common plant . . .

Answer Explanations

6 Connecting Content Question
(B) The professor talks about the amount of sunlight that the Arctic gets in both summer and winter.

7 Detail Question
Fact: 2, 3   Not a Fact: 1, 4
In the lecture, the professor says, "To adapt to this problem, most Arctic plants are short and squat, so they grow low to the ground, which enables them to avoid being ripped out of the soil by the wind." Then, she comments, "Furthermore, Arctic plants typically grow very close together, which provides them with added protection from the wind." She does not say that their roots can grow into the permafrost; she says the opposite. And Arctic plants do not have long and broad leaves.

8 Detail Question
(A) About Arctic moss, the professor lectures, "It grows in thick carpets, which helps keep the land warmer, which, in turn, allows other plants to grow."

9 Understanding Organization Question
(B) In talking about the Inuit people, the professor remarks, "The diamond leaf willow is highly prized by the Inuit people as its leaves are a rich source of vitamin C."

10 Making Inferences Question
(A) At the end of the lecture, the professor says, "Okay, let's look at another common plant." So she will probably show the students a picture and talk about it like she has been doing.

11 Understanding Attitude Question
(C) In stating, "It's practically a miracle that any plants live in the Arctic at all," the professor means that the conditions in the Arctic are poor and are not good for most plants.

PART 1 Lecture #2

Script

Listen to part of a lecture in a chemistry class.

M Professor: In ancient times, humans only knew about nine of the elements which are on the periodic chart. They were aware of gold, silver, copper, iron, mercury, lead, carbon, sulfur, and tin. By the seventeenth century, four more elements—arsenic, antimony, phosphorus, and zinc—had been discovered. Then, in the eighteenth century, when people were learning more about science and their methods and equipment were improving, a large number of elements were discovered. I'd like to tell you about how three of them—hydrogen, oxygen, and nitrogen—were discovered so that you can understand how that happened.

I think we'll start with hydrogen. It's one of the most common elements, so most people would assume it was fairly easy to discover. However, hydrogen readily combines with other elements to form compounds, so it was only through experimentation that it was discovered. The first hint of the gas came in 1671 when English chemist Robert Boyle published a paper on the relationship between flame and air. In one of his experiments, he witnessed a reaction between iron filings and diluted acids, and he noticed a gas being given off, but he failed to understand what exactly was happening. Boyle had found hydrogen, but he didn't know what it was. Interestingly, it took almost a century before somebody else became aware of it. That man was Henry Cavendish, another English chemist. In 1766, he was experimenting with mercury and acids when he noticed a gaseous substance being formed. He recorded its properties and called it inflammable air. The name hydrogen

Actual Test 06   **37**

came from Frenchman Antoine Lavoisier, who essentially repeated Cavendish's experiments with metals and acids in 1783. Since Cavendish did the initial experiments, most science books credit him, not Lavoisier, with discovering hydrogen though.

Let's move on to nitrogen, which was discovered by Scottish doctor Daniel Rutherford in 1772. During his time, there was a widespread belief that air had two main parts: One was highly combustible and reactive while the other was very inert and nonreactive and would extinguish flames and kill small animals. Rutherford observed this inert gas during some of his experiments. He called it noxious air, but it was later referred to as nitrogen by French chemist Jean-Antoine Chaptal in 1790.

The second part of air, uh, the reactive part, was oxygen. In the late 1600s, Robert Boyle had deduced that air was needed to make the reaction that caused fire, but he never knew the reason. So who discovered oxygen . . . ? Hmm . . . that's a good question. There are three candidates: Swede Carl Wilhelm Scheele, Englishman Joseph Priestley, and Frenchman Antoine Lavoisier.

Scheele discovered oxygen in 1772 yet didn't publish his work until 1777. Even today, a person isn't said to have discovered something until the findings are made public. This was a problem because, um, Joseph Priestley independently discovered oxygen in 1774 and published the results of his experiment immediately. Later, Priestley visited Lavoisier, where the two discussed chemistry. Then, in 1775, Lavoisier announced that he had independently discovered oxygen, which caused Priestley to claim that the Frenchman had picked his brain and stolen his discovery. There was something of a controversy at the time, but Scheele and Priestley are often jointly credited with discovering oxygen while Lavoisier's claim is viewed with skepticism. Lavoisier did, however, contribute by coining the word oxygen, which we use to describe the element.

W Student: How did Scheele and Priestley independently arrive at the same idea? Did they conduct the same experiments?

M: The experiments were similar, and there's also no evidence that the two men were in contact with each other, so that's why we say they independently discovered it.

W: What were their experiments like?

M: Scheele experimented by heating different metal compounds. Whenever he burned the metals, he noticed that a gas was produced. He collected some of the gas, and, when it came into contact with charcoal dust, it made some brilliant sparks. Scheele called the gas, um, fire air

. . . Yeah, that wasn't very creative, was it? As for Priestley, he too experimented with burning metals and collected the gas produced in glass containers. After more experiments, he noted that the gas made flames burn more intensely and kept small animals alive for a long time. Priestley concluded that he had found a new gas.

Ah, let me tell you something important regarding the history of science. During Priestley's time, one popular theory was that when something burned, it broke down into two parts. One was a gas, and the other was the ash left over. Scientists called this the phlogiston theory, and the gases given off by flammable materials were called phlogiston. Er . . . that's spelled P-H-L-O-G-I-S-T-O-N in case you don't know. Priestley was a strong believer in this theory, yet he concluded that the new gas had no phlogiston, so he called it dephlogisticated air. Lavoisier, however, said that there was no such thing as phlogiston and that the air was made up of different elements, including nitrogen and oxygen. His theory, as we know today, proved to be correct.

Answer Explanations

12 Gist-Content Question

(C) The professor tells the students about how people used various scientific methods to discover three elements.

13 Understanding Organization Question

(A) About Boyle, the professor notes, "The first hint of the gas came in 1671 when English chemist Robert Boyle published a paper on the relationship between flame and air. In one of his experiments, he witnessed a reaction between iron filings and diluted acids, and he noticed a gas being given off, but he failed to understand what exactly was happening. Boyle had found hydrogen, but he didn't know what it was."

14 Detail Question

(B) The professor states, "Let's move on to nitrogen, which was discovered by Scottish doctor Daniel Rutherford in 1772."

15 Connecting Content Question

Hydrogen: 1, 2   Oxygen: 3, 4

About hydrogen, the professor comments, "That man was Henry Cavendish, another English chemist. In 1766, he was experimenting with mercury and acids when he noticed a gaseous substance being formed. He recorded its properties and called it inflammable air." Regarding oxygen, he states, "Whenever he burned the metals, he noticed that a gas was produced. He collected some of the gas, and, when it came into contact with charcoal dust, it made some brilliant sparks. Scheele called the gas, um, fire air . . . Yeah, that wasn't very creative, was it? As for Priestley, he too experimented with burning metals and collected the gas produced in glass containers. After more experiments, he noted that the gas made flames burn more intensely."

16 Understanding Function Question

(B) The female student asks the professor about Scheele's experiments, so he responds by describing them.

17 Understanding Organization Question

(D) The professor talks about the discovery of each element individually.

PART 2 Conversation
p. 110

Script

Listen to part of a conversation between a student and a professor.

M Student: Professor Donaldson, I have a question. It, uh, concerns something you mentioned in today's class. You claimed the Roman Empire existed during the Middle Ages, but I was under the impression that it fell during the fifth century. What exactly were you talking about?

W Professor: Good query, Fred. I was talking about the Eastern Roman Empire, which lasted until the year 1453.

M: The Eastern Roman Empire? Um . . . I've never heard of that.

W: How about the Byzantine Empire?

M: I recall my high school history teacher saying something about it, but, uh, to be honest, I wasn't the most attentive student back then. Would you mind giving me a brief lesson? I guess this will be on our midterm exam.

W: Good guess. In addition, it's something you should know since the Byzantine Empire wasn't just one of history's greatest empires, but it also carried on the legacy of Rome for centuries after Rome was conquered by Western barbarians.

M: It sounds fascinating. So, uh, what happened?

W: Well, before discussing the Byzantine Empire, I should say a few things about the Roman Empire. But first, how about telling me what you know about the Roman Empire?

M: Hmm . . . It was one of the most powerful and biggest empires ever. At its height, which I believe was during the

second century, it occupied most of Western Europe, parts of Britain, land in Eastern and Northern Europe, Asia Minor, parts of the Middle East, and large amounts of land in North Africa.

W: So you do know a bit about Rome. And, um, yes, the size of the empire was impressive. In fact, it became so big that it was impossible for one man to run. In addition, during the third century, the empire underwent crisis after crisis. Emperors were constantly assassinated, generals rebelled, there were economic problems, and foreigners also invaded.

M: It sounds like a recipe for disaster. What happened?

W: We'll get into that in next week's lecture, but let me give you the short version. Emperor Claudius II started stabilizing the empire around 270 A.D. But he died before enacting all of his plans. Then, the big change happened in 286 under Emperor Diocletian.

M: I think I've heard of him.

W: Diocletian split the empire into two halves and created the Western Roman Empire and the Eastern Roman Empire. He hoped this would make the administration of the empire easier. However, the Western Roman Empire went into decline while the Eastern Roman Empire became more powerful.

M: And the Eastern Roman Empire was the Byzantine Empire?

W: Correct. Constantine the Great established the Byzantine Empire in the year 330. Its capital was Constantinople, which is the modern-day city of Istanbul, Turkey. The Byzantine Empire would last for more than a thousand years. It protected the people of Europe from numerous invaders during that time, and it also preserved copious amounts of knowledge from ancient Greece and Rome. Thanks to the Byzantines, this learning would later spread to Europe and spark the Renaissance.

M: Thank you so much for that history lesson, ma'am. I'll go to the library to check out some books on the topic just as soon as my next class ends. If I have any more questions, I'll let you know. I've got to run now, or I'm going to be late.

Answer Explanations

1 Gist-Purpose Question

(B) At the start of the conversation, the student says, "Professor Donaldson, I have a question. It, uh, concerns something you mentioned in today's class. You claimed the Roman Empire existed during the Middle Ages, but I was under the impression that it fell during the fifth century. What exactly were you talking about?"

2 Making Inferences Question

(D) It can be inferred that the student was not diligent in high school when he remarks, "I recall my high school history teacher saying something about it, but, uh, to be honest, I wasn't the most attentive student back then."

3 Understanding Function Question

(C) The professor wants to know how much knowledge the student has about the Roman Empire when she asks the student about it.

4 Detail Question

1, 3 The professor states, "The Byzantine Empire would last for more than a thousand years. It protected the people of Europe from numerous invaders during that time, and it also preserved copious amounts of knowledge from ancient Greece and Rome."

5 Making Inferences Question

(B) The student indicates he has a class to attend now by saying, "I'll go to the library to check out some books on the topic just as soon as my next class ends. If I have any more questions, I'll let you know. I've got to run now, or I'm going to be late."

PART 2 Lecture

p. 113

Script

Listen to part of a lecture in an art history class.

W1 Professor: Let's move on to another artist. Take a close look at these pictures here . . . and here . . . and here. And, um, here's another one for you . . . 🎧11 Can anyone tell me who painted these pictures . . . ? Yes, you with your hand up in the third row . . .

W2 Student: I'm not positive, but they look like some of the paintings of Edgar Degas.

W1: That's an excellent guess as the artist we're going to study was indeed influenced by Degas, but I'm afraid that he didn't paint those pictures. Would anyone else care to hazard a guess . . . ? No . . . ? Okay, I'll tell you then. Those pictures were painted by Mary Cassatt. That's C-A-S-S-A-T-T. Mary Cassatt was an American painter who's often associated with the Impressionist school of France. She's primarily known for her large collection of paintings depicting female subjects. Like this . . . and this . . . She frequently painted young girls alone . . . as well as mothers and their children together . . . Here's another one . . . Most of these paintings showed common everyday aspects of life, including, um, sleeping . . . bathing . . . feeding . . . and playing outdoors . . . In many of her works, Mary Cassatt portrayed the love and bond between mother and child as they hug . . . or hold each other closely . . . Cassatt may not be as well-known as other painters of the nineteenth century, but she was clearly one of the best of that period. Even today, her paintings continue to influence many artists.

Now, uh, let's back up a bit so that I can give you some details about her early life. Cassatt was born in the United States in 1844 but spent most of her adult life in Europe—mainly France—where she became friends and colleagues with great artists such as Edgar Degas, whom we just mentioned. She came from a well-to-do Pennsylvania family and traveled in Europe as child, where, uh, in France, she first became exposed to the vibrant art world that she later joined. In the U.S., despite her parents' objections, she studied art at a professional school. However, she became frustrated by the plodding pace of instruction and the domination of the school by the male instructors and students. Mary decided she'd never learn to be a great painter unless she studied in France, which was considered the center of the art world in the mid-1800s. Therefore, in 1866, she moved to Paris to begin studying intensively. This act had a profound influence on her life.

Mary spent two years studying privately with different artists and also studied drawing and painting by copying the works of the masters on display in the Louvre. In 1868, one of her paintings was selected to be displayed in the famous Paris Salon, a yearly exhibition sponsored by the French government. The work was called *A Mandolin Player*. Uh, here it is . . . As you can clearly see, this painting was done in the Romantic style. In spite of the enormous achievement of having a painting selected for display in the Paris Salon, real success eluded her, and, when the Franco-Prussian War broke out in 1870, she reluctantly headed home. In the U.S., Mary's father, who disapproved of her activities, cut her off financially. However, her fortunes changed for the better when she was commissioned to make copies of some Italian masterpieces for the archbishop of the Catholic Church in Pittsburgh. With funds in her pockets again, she set off for Italy to study those works of art. From then on, she spent most of the remainder of her life in Europe. Her paintings were again selected for the Paris Salon, and she began receiving the respect of the French art world she had long desired.

M Student: Didn't the Paris Salon object to Impressionism though? I thought Cassatt was an Impressionist.

W1: Not initially, she wasn't. It was only later in her life that

Mary became frustrated by the restrictions of the Paris Salon. You see, class, the Paris Salon had guidelines artists had to follow to have their works accepted. In the 1860s and 1870s, when Impressionism was just beginning, the Paris Salon was against that style. It was during that period that Mary came under the influence of Edgar Degas. She began using more vibrant colors and pastels in imitation of his style. Despite being criticized for doing that, she met Degas and became his student. From him, she learned to etch and to be a proficient drawer. Thanks to his tutelage, in 1879, she put on an exhibition of her works and was then fully accepted by the Impressionists of the time.

Around the same time, her works started being dominated by female subjects. Additionally, her style began to change, so, by the 1890s, she had created a style that was pretty much all her own. Notice here . . . how she used a more realistic style of painting portraits of women and children. She also started using more muted and realistic colors, like you can see here . . . and here . . . Sadly, she contracted diabetes late in life and gradually lost her sight. From 1914 until her death in France in 1926, she didn't paint or draw a single picture.

Answer Explanations

6 Gist-Content Question

Ⓒ During the lecture, the professor focuses upon the different styles that Mary Cassatt painted in during her life.

7 Understanding Attitude Question

Ⓑ About Mary Cassatt, the professor comments, "Cassatt may not be as well-known as other painters of the nineteenth century, but she was clearly one of the best of that period."

8 Detail Question

Ⓓ The professor states, "In 1868, one of her paintings was selected to be displayed in the famous Paris Salon, a yearly exhibition sponsored by the French government. The work was called *A Mandolin Player*. Uh, here it is . . . As you can clearly see, this painting was done in the Romantic style. In spite of the enormous achievement of having a painting selected for display in the Paris Salon, real success eluded her."

9 Detail Question

Fact: 1, 2, 4   Not a Fact: 3
First, the professor states, "In the U.S., despite her parents' objections, she studied art at a professional school," and she also says, "In the U.S., Mary's father,

who disapproved of her activities, cut her off financially." Next, the professor notes that Mary Cassatt was both a Romantic and Impressionist painter. Finally, the professor tells the students, "From 1914 until her death in France in 1926, she didn't paint or draw a single picture." The professor does not, however, remark that Mary Cassatt never lacked funds because she sold a lot of paintings.

10 Making Inferences Question

Ⓐ About Edgar Degas, the professor notes, "It was during that period that Mary came under the influence of Edgar Degas. She began using more vibrant colors and pastels in imitation of his style. Despite being criticized for doing that, she met Degas and became his student. From him, she learned to etch and to be a proficient drawer. Thanks to his tutelage, in 1879, she put on an exhibition of her works and was then fully accepted by the Impressionists of the time." It can therefore be inferred that Edgar Degas helped Mary Cassatt join the Impressionist Movement.

11 Understanding Function Question

Ⓓ When the professor says, "I'm afraid that he didn't paint those pictures," in response to the student's comment that the pictures look like those of Edgar Degas, she is indicating that the student gave an incorrect answer.

Actual Test 07

ANSWERS

PART 1

1 Ⓒ	2 Ⓐ	3 Ⓓ	4 ③, ④	5 Ⓑ
6 Ⓑ	7 Ⓐ	8 cause: ②	Effect: ①, ③, ④	
9 Ⓒ	10 Ⓒ	11 Ⓓ		

PART 2

1 Ⓓ	2 ①, ③	3 Ⓑ	4 Ⓓ	5 Ⓑ
6 Ⓑ	7 ③, ④			
8 Sugar: ③	Starch: ①	Fiber: ②, ④		
9 Ⓑ	10 Ⓐ	11 Ⓒ	12 Ⓑ	13 Ⓐ
14 Ⓒ	15 Android: ③, ④	Cyborg: ①, ②		
16 Ⓑ	17 Ⓐ			

PART 1 Conversation

p. 119

Script

Listen to part of a conversation between a student and a professor.

W Student: Professor Wagner, have you reviewed the outline I submitted for my class presentation? I know I don't have to give it until two weeks from now, but I'd like to make sure everything is fine. There are still a few things left for me to, uh, to research, and I also plan to make some slides to show while I speak.

M Professor: It sounds like an ambitious project, Cindy. I'm glad to hear you're so interested in doing the work.

W: Thank you, sir.

M: And, uh, as a matter of fact, I did check the outline last night.

W: Great. Any thoughts?

M: A few. I think your topic of sexual dimorphism is pretty interesting. May I ask why you decided on it?

W: I've always been curious about why males and females of many species look different from one another. Uh, I mean, aside from the differences in their reproductive organs. So I thought it would be interesting to find out why sexual dimorphism happens.

M: Yes, it's an interesting topic, isn't it?

W: It sure is.

M: Well, I liked some of your examples. Obviously, you chose the peacock and the peahen to illustrate sexual dimorphism. The peacock has much flashier feathers than the female. You might also consider using the bird of paradise as another example. Males are much more colorful than females.

W: Okay, I'll check that out. Thank you.

M: However, uh, I must take exception to your claim that the sole reason for sexual dimorphism is reproductive purposes.

W: Oh? Why is that?

M: First, you're not totally wrong. I mean, animals such as the peacock and the bird of paradise have males and females that look different merely for reproductive purposes. But that's not always the case. Hmm . . . I recently read an article about an insect called the orchid mantis. As its name suggests, it closely resembles an orchid in appearance. Males of the species are approximately 2.5 centimeters long whereas females can grow to be six or seven centimeters in length.

W: Wow. Why is there such a big difference?

M: Hunting. Males are quite skittish, probably on account of their small size. Females, however, are more aggressive thanks to their impressive length. And because they're so big, they eat much more than males.

W: That makes sense.

M: So I'd like you to reconsider your analysis of sexual dimorphism. Use the orchid mantis as an example and find a couple of other similar examples. If you do that, I'm pretty sure you'll receive an A.

W: That sounds perfect, sir. Oh, uh, before I go, would you happen to recall where you read the article about the orchid mantis? I'd love to get my hands on it. And are there any other animals that you'd recommend including in my presentation?

M: Let me see . . . Ah, here's the magazine I found it in. Go ahead and take it. Just copy the pages the article is in and return it to me tomorrow before class starts. When you read the article, you'll notice the author mentions some animals in addition to the orchid mantis but doesn't go into detail on them, so this article should be all you need to get started on your research.

Answer Explanations

1 Gist-Content Question

Ⓒ Most of the conversation involves the student and

the professor discussing an outline for a paper that the student turned in to the professor.

2 Understanding Function Question

(A) About the bird of paradise, the professor remarks, "You might also consider using the bird of paradise as another example. Males are much more colorful than females."

3 Understanding Attitude Question

(D) First, the professor states, "However, uh, I must take exception to your claim that the sole reason for sexual dimorphism is reproductive purposes." Then, he adds, "First, please be aware that you're not totally wrong. I mean, animals such as the peacock and the bird of paradise have males and females that look different merely for reproductive purposes. But that's not always the case." So his opinion is that the student has an incorrect opinion about one aspect of sexual dimorphism.

4 Detail Question

3 , 4 The professor points out, "Males are quite skittish, probably on account of their small size. Females, however, are more aggressive thanks to their impressive length. And because they're so big, they eat much more than males."

5 Connecting Content Question

(B) The professor comments, "When you read the article, you'll notice the author mentions some animals in addition to the orchid mantis but doesn't go into detail on them, so this article should be all you need to get started on your research." So a likely outcome of the student reading the article is that she will learn about some examples she can use for her presentation.

PART 1 Lecture
p. 122

Script

Listen to part of a lecture in a musicology class.

W Professor: For a few decades from the, hmm . . . from the 1920s to the 1940s I suppose, the radio dominated the home entertainment field. But one thing people couldn't do was program the radio to play what they wanted. They had to rely on the musical choices of the DJs working at the radio stations instead. As a result, when people wanted to listen to specific songs, they played vinyl records at their homes. Naturally, most people had limited selections of music at their homes. Then along came the jukebox, which was a machine containing recorded music, and it

dramatically changed people's listening habits.

The jukebox evolved from the mechanical music players of the 1800s and early 1900s. The classic one was the mechanical piano player, which had a roll of paper with slots or bumps that, when played, would hit all the proper notes to play a song on the piano. I'm sure everyone has seen video of one, right . . . ? Okay, I see heads nodding. That's good. Well, after Thomas Edison developed the first device that could record sound, mechanical piano players transformed into machines that could play early wax recordings. Then, in the United States in 1928, the first jukebox was made. It could play eight different records.

M Student: Pardon the interruption, but where does the name jukebox come from?

W: I think the word box is obvious since it was shaped like a box. As for juke, that word comes from the term juke joint, which was a type of club which played lively music during that time. Eventually, jukeboxes became coin-operated machines that let people press buttons to select the music they wanted to hear. It typically cost a nickel to play a few songs, but, as time went by, prices rose. I remember when I was a teen back in the 1980s that you could get three songs for a quarter on some machines.

Anyway, by the 1940s, the jukebox had become popular around the country, and it had its heyday in the 1950s and 1960s. Over time, it evolved into an elaborate machine with chrome and colorful glass fittings as well as lots of flashing lights. Jukeboxes could be found in many places, but they were typically set up in bars, restaurants, and dance clubs. In some establishments, there was a small machine at each table which let customers select songs. I suppose that was sort of like an early version of a remote control. Some of those remote machines could even let the people at one table listen to a song while the people at the next table over got to hear a different one.

So, um . . . what's the connection with radio . . . ? Well, the jukebox started to replace radios in bars, restaurants, and dance clubs, and many people frequently left their homes at night and went to establishments with jukeboxes where they could listen to music. As a result, the number of radio listeners declined. This hurt the radio business since radio stations depended upon advertising for money, and, because fewer people were listening, their advertisers wound up spending less money.

Basically, the jukebox had several advantages over the radio. First, people could select the music they wanted to hear, and they didn't have to listen to any commercials or news reports. In addition, in the 1950s and 1960s, young people mostly wanted to hear the latest songs . . .

Remember that this was when Elvis Presley, the Beatles, and other musicians were incredibly popular . . . By this time, the technology had improved so that there might have been hundreds of songs in a single jukebox, which ensured that the newest and most popular songs could be heard by people.

M: 🎧**11**What kind of records did jukeboxes play?

W: By the early 1950s, all jukebox music was recorded on small vinyl records called 45s because they played at 45 revolutions per minute.

M: Oh, I've seen those before in some old movies.

W: Yes, I know you all either download music or listen to CDs, but vinyl records were common up through the 1980s. I probably still have a few in my own music collection although I don't own a stereo any longer. Just so you know, at one point, roughly three-quarters of all vinyl record 45s manufactured in the U.S went into jukeboxes.

The owners of establishments with jukeboxes knew which songs were the most popular, so they replaced unpopular songs with popular ones to make more money. In time, the record companies caught on and started sending the newest records to places with jukeboxes. RCA, one of the big music companies back then, was among the first to see the advantage of doing that. RCA collected information about which singers, bands, and songs were popular and, interestingly, in which parts of the country they were popular, and then it used that data to make decisions on who and what to record and where to sell the recordings.

Overall, the jukebox was a great business model. It made money for the owners, the companies that built the machines, the music companies, and the performers. It did, however, hurt radio, so let's talk about that for a bit.

Answer Explanations

6 Understanding Function Question

Ⓑ The professor describes how the jukebox evolved by saying, "Well, after Thomas Edison developed the first device that could record sound, mechanical piano players transformed into machines that could play early wax recordings. Then, in the United States in 1928, the first jukebox was made."

7 Understanding Organization Question

Ⓐ The professor talks about RCA's business model involving jukeboxes when she remarks, "RCA, one of the big music companies back then, was among the first to see the advantage of doing that. RCA collected

information about which singers, bands, and songs were popular and, interestingly, in which parts of the country they were popular, and then it used that data to make decisions on who and what to record and where to sell the recordings."

8 Connecting Content Question

Cause: 2 **Effect:** 1, 3, 4

The professor points out that one cause of the popularity of the jukebox was that people wanted to hear certain songs, which they could do by playing them on the jukebox. As for the effects of the popularity of the jukebox, the professor states, "It did, however, hurt radio, so let's talk about that for a bit." She also notes, "Well, the jukebox started to replace radios in bars, restaurants, and dance clubs, and many people frequently left their homes at night and went to establishments with jukeboxes where they could listen to music." And she adds, "As a result, the number of radio listeners declined. This hurt the radio business since radio stations depended upon advertising for money, and, because fewer people were listening, their advertisers wound up spending less money."

9 Understanding Attitude Question

Ⓒ About the jukebox, the professor states, "Overall, the jukebox was a great business model. It made money for the owners, the companies that built the machines, the music companies, and the performers."

10 Making Inferences Question

Ⓒ In saying, "It did, however, hurt radio, so let's talk about that for a bit," at the end of the lecture, the professor indicates that she is going to change topics and start talking about a new one.

11 Understanding Attitude Question

Ⓓ When the student says that he has seen a vinyl record in old movies, he is implying that he has never played one before.

PART 2 Conversation p. 125

Script

Listen to part of a conversation between a student and a professor.

W Student: I really appreciate that suggestion, Professor Reynolds. Now that I've got a good idea on how to write my paper, I don't anticipate there being any other problems.

M Professor: That's great, Sheila. I'm glad I could be of assistance to you. So, um, is there anything else you'd like to speak with me about today? I believe there are a couple of other students waiting outside my office to talk to me. I don't want to keep them standing there for too much longer.

W: Oh, uh . . . Actually, if you don't mind, I need to talk about one more thing. To be honest, it's the real reason I came here to speak with you this afternoon.

M: Okay. What do you need to discuss?

W: It concerns summer vacation.

M: What about it?

W: Well, I stayed here at school and took classes and worked during the summer between my freshman and sophomore years as well as the one between my sophomore and junior years. I had part-time jobs on campus then. I'm planning to spend this coming summer here as well, but . . .

M: I'm sorry, but if you're asking if you can work for me, I'll be out of the country the entire summer, so I won't need any student assistants.

W: Oh, no. It's not that Professor Reynolds. You see, um, I'm hoping to get an internship, but I don't really know where to start.

M: Ah, an internship.

W: Yes, sir. I'm kind of curious if you have any ideas. I mean, uh, you used to work in the business sector before you became a professor here, right? So I'm guessing you might have some contacts or something.

M: Hmm . . . It's true that I still know a large number of people in the industry. In fact, I even do some consulting with them from time to time. As for internships, well, to be honest, I haven't heard anything about them. Of course, uh, I haven't had a reason to be paying attention to see if any companies are offering them.

W: You could find out though, couldn't you?

M: Yes, I suppose I could make a few phone calls. But I can't just single you out for special treatment, Sheila.

W: 🎧5What do you mean?

M: I mean that I'll talk to some people I know and find out if their companies need any interns. **Then, I'll make the announcement to all of the students in my class so that everyone has an equal opportunity to apply for them.** You're a good student, Sheila, and you'd make a great intern, but it would be wrong for me to show any favoritism to you.

W: That's perfectly understandable, sir. I don't mind competing against the other students. If someone more

qualified beats me out, well, uh, I can always get a part-time job on campus instead.

M: That's a very good attitude to have, Sheila. Nevertheless, if I can get some information about internships, I'm sure you'll have an excellent chance of being selected for one. After all, you're a straight-A student.

W: Thanks for saying that. I appreciate it. Anyway, uh, let me get going. I don't want to take up any more of your time.

M: All right. Thanks, Sheila. As soon as I speak with the students waiting outside, I'll call some people I know. I should be able to make an announcement to everyone during Friday's class.

Answer Explanations

1 Gist-Purpose Question

ⓓ The student mentions that she is going to be at the school during the summer, and then she comments, "You see, um, I'm hoping to get an internship, but I don't really know where to start," and asks him for assistance.

2 Detail Question

1, 3 The student says, "Well, I stayed here at school and took classes and worked during the summer between my freshman and sophomore years as well as the one between my sophomore and junior years. I had part-time jobs on campus then."

3 Understanding Function Question

ⓑ The student asks, "I mean, uh, you used to work in the business sector before you became a professor here, right? So I'm guessing you might have some contacts or something."

4 Understanding Attitude Question

ⓓ The professor remarks, "Nevertheless, if I can get some information about internships, I'm sure you'll have an excellent chance of being selected for one. After all, you're a straight-A student."

5 Understanding Attitude Question

ⓑ When the professor says that he wants everyone to have "an equal opportunity to apply for" the internships, he is indicating that he would like for every student to have the same chance to get an internship.

Script

Listen to part of a lecture in a physiology class.

W Professor: 🎧¹¹ You often hear people mention carbohydrates when they're speaking about their diets. There are many, uh, so-called experts who believe that eliminating carbohydrates, or carbs, as some people refer to them, is the key to losing weight. **Please don't be deceived by these individuals.** On the contrary, carbohydrates are a necessary part of a good diet. All right, uh, prior to speaking about how they can influence our health, I think I first need to tell you about the different types of carbohydrates and the functions of each of them.

Let me start by asking you a question . . . Do any of you know how many basic types of carbohydrates there are . . . ? No takers, huh . . . ? That's all right. To answer my own question, there are three basic types of carbohydrates: sugar, starch, and fiber. All three are found in the foods we eat, and all three are made of sugar molecules. We can further divide carbohydrates into simple and complex ones. Sugars are simple carbohydrates because they have only one or two molecules of sugar whereas starches and fibers are complex carbohydrates because they have many molecules of sugar—sometimes thousands of molecules in various forms. All of these carbohydrates enter our bodies through the food we eat. Then, in the digestive system, they are attacked by enzymes, which break them down. Eventually, even the most complex carbohydrates get transformed into simple sugars called monosaccharides. The reason this happens is that it's only in the form of simple sugars that carbohydrates can enter the bloodstream and be used as nutrition by the body.

There are three basic types of simple carbohydrates. They are sucrose, fructose, and lactose. Sucrose is found in the table sugar that people put in coffee and on top of cereal. Fructose gets its name from the fact that it's found in fruit while lactose is found in milk. You've probably heard of people who are lactose intolerant. It simply means they can't consume dairy products such as milk because their bodies have an adverse reaction to the lactose contained in milk. Numerous products with simple sugars are healthy food choices, but be aware that products with sucrose in them have been linked to dental diseases and put people at risk of getting diabetes.

Complex carbohydrates with starch come mainly from whole grains, peas, and beans. At first glance, these appear to be healthy foods. However, the modern-day food industry usually refines them in various ways, which is, frankly speaking, a problem. What happens is that processing wheat and other grains changes them from whole grains by removing the high-fiber parts of the kernels of the grains. That's how we get white flour, which is used to make white bread, pastas, and countless bakery products. Similar processing is done to rice to produce white rice. As a result, the complex starchy carbohydrates remain, but the healthy fiber is removed. So when you eat bread, rice, or pasta, your body gets a substantial shot of sugar but little in the way of fiber and vitamins. Naturally, this can have a negative impact on your health. Of course, it's possible to avoid processed grains, but it's not easy these days. You really have to watch what you eat carefully.

So this brings us to complex fiber carbohydrates, which are mainly found in vegetables, particularly leafy green vegetables such as lettuce, kale, and cabbage. These are some of the best food choices you can make because they have few calories and are rich in fiber, which assists with digestion. In addition, they contain plenty of vitamins and minerals and can keep the digestive tract clean and healthy. Eat as many of them as you like. Sadly, they aren't to everyone's taste, so not everyone eats them as much as they ought to.

At present, what we have is a modern-day health crisis. Simple carbohydrates and complex starchy carbohydrates are the leading causes of obesity and complications such as diabetes. By eating too many of the delicious, um, but not particularly nutritious foods, people get a sugar spike in their bodies. In essence, what happens is that the simple and starch carbohydrate-carrying foods many people consume are rich in sugars that get broken down easily, and then they pass through the liver and into the bloodstream. They provide a tremendous boost of energy, but it lasts only for a short time, and it comes with a, uh, a price. Once that energy boost is gone, a person's body crashes, so the individual will suddenly feel tired and listless. And it's only by eating more of those carbohydrates that the person can feel energetic again. That can lead to a rollercoaster ride for the body as its sugar levels spike and fall throughout the day. And it can cause various health-related issues, including diabetes, heart attacks, strokes, blindness, and the loss of feeling in the outer limbs.

Answer Explanations

6 Connecting Content Question

Ⓑ The professor states, "Numerous products with simple sugars are healthy food choices, but be aware that products with sucrose in them have been linked to dental diseases and put people at risk of getting diabetes." So a person who eats a lot of simple sugars will likely get diabetes.

7 Detail Question

3, 4 The professor states, "Complex carbohydrates with starch come mainly from whole grains, peas, and beans."

8 Connecting Content Question

Sugar: 3   Starch: 1   Fiber: 2, 4

Regarding sugar, the professor says, "There are three basic types of simple carbohydrates. They are sucrose, fructose, and lactose." As for starch, she comments, "Complex carbohydrates with starch come mainly from whole grains." And concerning fiber, she lectures, "So this brings us to complex fiber carbohydrates, which are mainly found in vegetables, particularly leafy green vegetables such as lettuce, kale, and cabbage. These are some of the best food choices you can make because they have few calories and are rich in fiber, which assists with digestion."

9 Making Inferences Question

B The professor comments, "At present, what we have is a modern-day health crisis. Simple carbohydrates and complex starchy carbohydrates are the leading causes of obesity and complications such as diabetes." Thus she implies that people can eat more fiber and less sugar and starch to overcome the crisis.

10 Understanding Organization Question

A During her lecture, the professor talks about three types of carbohydrates one at a time.

11 Understanding Function Question

C When the professor tells the students not to be deceived by what the people say, she is giving some advice to the students.

PART 2 Lecture #2   p. 131

Script

Listen to part of a lecture in a history of technology class.

M Professor: There are two terms which I'm positive all of you have heard of when people talk about robots. The terms are android and cyborg. Unfortunately, many people believe the two are equivalent, but that couldn't be further from the truth. In the most simplistic terms, an android is a machine . . . er, a robot, if you will . . . that's designed both to act and look like a human. On the other hand, a cyborg is a human—or an animal in some cases—that has machines which have replaced various parts of its body. In other words, a cyborg is partially organic and mechanical.

Those are two fairly simple explanations, so allow me to go into a few details for you. Uh, one thing you ought to be aware of is that most of these terms and definitions originated in either science-fiction literature or visual media, so let me give you some examples that come from them. Firstly, the word robot comes from a word in the Czech language that means "work" or "labor." It was first used in a play by the Czech writer Karel Capek in 1920. In his play, what he called robots actually more closely resembles what we refer to as androids today. Basically, uh, Capek's robots were machines that resembled humans and were constructed to do labor. Since then, however, the term robot has come to be applied to virtually any machine that can do sophisticated work automatically after some initial programming. By the end of the twentieth century, such robots were commonplace in factories where repetitive motions were required to do precision work. Automobile factories in particular make use of robots nowadays.

🎧17 Thus a robot is a machine that does work, and, well, so is an android. Therefore all androids are robots, but not all robots are androids. **That's an important distinction which you all need to be aware of.** The reason not all robots are androids is that not all robots resemble humans, and, as I just mentioned, a machine must be humanlike to be considered an android. Again, while Capek's robots were in fact androids, he didn't use the term despite the fact that it had already been coined prior to the writing of his play. The term android was initially used in the nineteenth century and has its roots in the Greek language. It basically means, um, "a thing looking like a man." Its first noticeable usage was in a French book called *Tomorrow's Eve*, which was published in, uh, 1886 I believe. During the twentieth century, the term android became popular and was widely used in science-fiction novels, comic books, TV shows, and movies.

W Student: Yeah, wasn't that term used in *Star Wars* to refer to the androids in it?

M: Ah, actually, according to the commonly accepted definitions, George Lucas used the term improperly. You see, the two most famous robots in *Star Wars* were R2-D2 and C3PO. You're all familiar with them, right . . . ? Good . . . In the film, they were both referred to as droids, which is a shortened form of android. Nevertheless, those two machines were clearly robots. Well, um, I suppose an argument could be made that C3PO was vaguely human looking as it was bipedal and had some facial features and a voice that resembled that of a human. However, C3PO had no skin texture, no human eyes, and, well, nothing that could make it pass for a human.

The same cannot be said of Lieutenant Commander Data, a character on one of the *Star Trek* spinoffs in the 1980s and 1990s, though. Data was an android, so he was a machine that looked and acted human. Of course, he was played by a human actor and wasn't the real thing. But, um, nowadays, we do have the real thing. In Japan and Korea, researchers are doing marvelous work creating androids that are quite realistically human. These androids have facial movements which mimic human emotions and can even respond to standard questions by using realistic human voices. While these androids are still relatively primitive in the grand scheme of things, in the future, it may be difficult to tell androids and humans apart.

What about cyborgs . . . ? First, to reiterate, a cyborg is a living thing with mechanical parts. The term is a combination of the words cybernetic and organism. The concept of a human with mechanical parts was popular in science fiction throughout the twentieth century, but the word cyborg only originated in a scientific journal in 1960. Two writers, Manfred Clynes and Nathan Kline, wrote an article about the role humans would play in space exploration for the journal *Astronautics*. The two authors proposed that an enhanced human being, which they called a cyborg, would be needed to survive the rigors of space. What a cyborg is, uh, is something of a gray area. Why? Well, is a man with an artificial leg a cyborg . . . ? I'd say yes only if the leg isn't just a simple prosthetic but is instead an enhanced machine that can mimic how humans walk. Let me give you some examples from popular movies so that you can understand more clearly what a cyborg is.

robots in *Star Wars* were R2-D2 and C3 PO. You're all familiar with them, right . . . ? Good . . . In the film, they were both referred to as droids, which is a shortened form of android. Nevertheless, those two machines were clearly robots."

15 Connecting Content Question

Android: ③, ④   Cyborg: ①, ②

About androids, the professor comments, "The term android was initially used in the nineteenth century and has its roots in the Greek language," and, "The reason not all robots are androids is that not all robots resemble humans, and, as I just mentioned, a machine must be humanlike to be considered an android." Regarding cyborgs, the professor tells the class, "A cyborg is a living thing with mechanical parts," and, "a cyborg is a human—or an animal in some cases—that has machines which have replaced various parts of its body."

16 Making Inferences Question

Ⓑ At the end of the lecture, the professor comments, "Let me give you some examples from popular movies so that you can understand more clearly what a cyborg is." So the professor will probably continue lecturing on cyborgs.

17 Understanding Function Question

Ⓐ When the professor tells the students that they need to be aware of a distinction that he is making, he is telling them that to emphasize a point he is making.

Answer Explanations

12 Gist-Content Question

Ⓑ The professor spends most of the lecture describing how androids and cyborgs are both similar to and different from one another.

13 Understanding Organization Question

Ⓐ The professor lectures, "Firstly, the word robot comes from a word in the Czech language that means "work" or "labor." It was first used in a play by the Czech writer Karel Capek in 1920."

14 Detail Question

Ⓒ The professor remarks, "Ah, actually, according to the commonly accepted definitions, George Lucas used the term improperly. You see, the two most famous

ANSWERS

PART 1

1 ⓒ	2 ⓓ	3 ⓐ	4 ⓒ	5 ⓐ
6 ⓑ	7 ⓓ	8 ⓒ	9 ⓑ	10 ⓓ
11 ⓐ	12 ⓒ	13 ⓐ	14 ②, ④	
15 ⓑ	16 ⓓ	17 ⓒ		

PART 2

1 ⓓ	2 ⓓ	3 ①, ②	4 ⓑ	5 ⓐ
6 ⓑ	7 ⓑ	8 ⓓ		
9 Fact: ②, ③ Not a Fact: ①, ④				
10 ⓑ	11 ⓒ			

PART 1 Conversation

p. 137

Script

Listen to part of a conversation between a student and a dormitory resident assistant.

M1 Student: Hey, Fred, do you have a moment to spare?

M2 Dormitory Resident Assistant: Sure, Tim, what's up?

M1: I need to discuss the upcoming final exam period with you. I'm specifically referring to the school's regulations concerning how quiet everyone in the dorm needs to be.

M2: Do you need me to explain the rules about that? They're pretty simple.

M1: No, I'm familiar with how quiet we need to be. I love the idea the school came up with that everyone has to be extremely quiet in the dorms for twenty-three hours a day. I think that's pretty cool.

M2: Yes, I fully agree with you. And the one hour when students can be as loud as they want is kind of fun. It's a great time to let off some steam.

M1: Yeah, that's true.

M2: Anyway, if you understand the rules, then what do you need to talk to me about?

M1: Basically, I need to make sure you're going to enforce the rules during the quiet period.

M2: Huh? Of course I'm going to. It's my job as an RA to do that. What makes you think I wouldn't?

M1: Well, Terry and Paul in room 304 have been making noise at all hours of the day and night this semester, but you haven't done anything about them despite the fact that several students—not just me—have complained to you about them. 🎧⁵Those guys have been driving me and almost everyone else on this floor crazy, but you just, uh, you just ignore them.

M2: I don't think they've been too loud this semester.

M1: Are you serious? Fred, they woke up half the dormitory last night when they suddenly started blasting rock music at three in the morning. You aren't trying to tell me that you didn't hear that, are you?

M2: Actually, um, I didn't hear anything. Honest. My room is at the other end of the hallway, so I must have slept right through it. Why did you wait to tell me about that until right now?

M1: What's the point? Many of us have complained repeatedly this semester, but you haven't fined them, and I don't believe you've even spoken with them once.

M2: I knocked on their door a few times, but they weren't around.

M1: That's not sufficient, Fred. You'd better have a long chat with Terry and Paul before the quiet period starts. All of the guys on this floor are fed up with them. If they make any noise during that period, we're going to visit the student housing office and file a complaint. We're also going to mention that you're the RA and that you haven't done a single thing to keep them quiet.

M2: Whoa . . . Slow down, Tim. You don't want to do that. I'll go over there right now and speak to them. I'll make sure they don't disturb your studies. If they make any noise, just come and talk to me, and I'll straighten them out.

M1: I seriously doubt they'll listen to you, but they're in their room now. I saw them getting back from their classes a few minutes ago.

M2: Okay, thanks for the tip. And don't worry about a thing, Tim. I've got this matter handled.

Answer Explanations

1 **Gist-Content Question**

ⓒ Most of the conversation involves the speakers talking about Terry and Paul, two students in the dormitory who have been bothering the other students.

2 **Understanding Attitude Question**

ⓓ The student notes, "Terry and Paul in room 304

have been making noise at all hours of the day and night this semester."

3 Making Inferences Question

(A) The student says, "If they make any noise during that period, we're going to visit the student housing office and file a complaint. We're also going to mention that you're the RA and that you haven't done a single thing to keep them quiet." The resident assistant then responds, "You don't want to do that." Thus it can be inferred that he does not want the students to file a complaint.

4 Making Inferences Question

(C) The student says that Terry and Paul are currently in their room, and the resident assistant indicates that he will go there to speak with them.

5 Understanding Function Question

(A) The resident assistant says that Terry and Paul have not been too loud, and the student responds by asking, "Are you serious?" He is therefore expressing his disbelief at what the resident assistant says.

PART 1 Lecture #1 p. 140

Script

Listen to part of a lecture in an American literature class.

W Professor: Okay, we've got a lot to cover this morning, so please take your seats so that we can get started . . . Thank you . . . Mark Twain is arguably America's most famous author as well as its greatest humorist. He was born in 1835 in the town of Florida, Missouri, and his parents gave him the name Samuel Langhorne Clemens. His family later moved to the town of Hannibal, Missouri, which was situated by the Mississippi River. In Hannibal, young Samuel was exposed to the world of riverboats and all of the colorful aspects of riverboat life. Samuel spent some time working on a riverboat when he was a young man. Um . . . I believe he did that for around three years. It was while he was working on the riverboat that he came up with his penname. When a boat was in shallow water, the crew would sink a lead-weighted line into the water to measure its depth. When it reached two fathoms, uh, about four meters of water, the man with the line would call out, "Mark Twain." Twain, you see, was the term used for two fathoms of water. So that's why we call him Mark Twain today.

In 1861, the Civil War began, and that brought Twain's riverboat career to an abrupt end since the Mississippi River was basically closed to riverboat traffic. Twain served a short stint as a volunteer soldier, but he quickly decided he wanted nothing to do with the war. As a result, in 1861, he moved west and got jobs at various newspapers in Nevada and, um, in California and Hawaii later. As a newspaper writer, he began what was to become a lifelong tradition of writing humorously about the events of the day. It was also during this period, um, in 1863, that he abandoned his birth name and began going by the penname Mark Twain. Only a few years after becoming a writer, he scored his first major success with the short story "The Celebrated Jumping Frog of Calaveras County," which he wrote in 1865.

After the Civil War ended in that same year, Twain took a long overseas journey to Europe and the Middle East. Based on his experiences in those place, he wrote a humorous book about Americans traveling entitled *The Innocents Abroad*. It was published in 1869. Upon his return to the United States, he married Olivia Langdon in 1870, and the two settled down in Hartford, Connecticut, where they raised three daughters. For the next twenty years, Twain had his most productive writing period. He continually wrote articles for both newspapers and magazines, and his writing was in great demand. With the money he earned from those articles, he was able to spend the rest of his time writing novels. He often chose to write about his boyhood experiences on the Mississippi River.

🎧**11** They served as the basis for his two greatest novels, *The Adventures of Tom Sawyer*, which was published in 1876, and *The Adventures of Huckleberry Finn*, which came out in 1885. I'd like to spend a few moments now discussing the writing style Twain used in *Huckleberry Finn*. **By the way, you should all be reading *Huckleberry Finn*, uh, or be finished with it, by now, so I'm sure questions about the book and Twain's writing style are on your mind.** I don't doubt that many of you may be struggling with the book. Don't be alarmed. I had problems with it as well when I first read it around, oh, three decades ago. Personally, I hated it then and still occasionally have problems with the language used today. The reason is that Twain didn't write the book in the standard fashion. Instead, he wrote using what is known as colloquialisms. His prose—especially his dialogue—reflects the way that the locals spoke. Since he was writing about the land he lived in during his youth, he chose to write in the dialect of the people who lived alongside and worked on the Mississippi River.

Now, um, as for colloquialisms . . . Authors use them out of a desire to capture the essence of how certain people act, think, and speak. Colloquial language is dramatically different than Standard English, uh, what's known as the Queen's English. In the nineteenth century, it was common for novelists to have characters speaking as though they were in a high-society salon. That was the fashion since most of the people reading the books belonged to the upper class. But during the 1800s, the mass education of the time resulted in an increase in the literacy rate, so more and more people began reading. As a result, much of the writing reflected the common lives of everyday people. This realism, as it was called, was found not only in literature but also in art, staged plays, and, years later, the cinema. In American literature, Twain led the way with his depictions of realism in common people's lives. Here, uh, let me give you a couple of examples before I finish giving you his biographical details.

Answer Explanations

6 Gist-Content Question

Ⓑ The professor spends most of the lecture telling the students about the important events in Mark Twain's life.

7 Understanding Function Question

Ⓓ The professor explains the origin of the penname Mark Twain when she notes, "Samuel spent some time working on a riverboat when he was a young man. Um . . . I believe he did that for around three years. It was while he was working on the riverboat that he came up with his penname. When a boat was in shallow water, the crew would sink a lead-weighted line into the water to measure its depth. When it reached two fathoms, uh, about four meters of water, the man with the line would call out, "Mark Twain." Twain, you see, was the term used for two fathoms of water. So that's why we call him Mark Twain today."

8 Detail Question

Ⓒ The professor tells the students, "Only a few years after becoming a writer, he scored his first major success with the short story 'The Celebrated Jumping Frog of Calaveras County.'"

9 Understanding Attitude Question

Ⓑ Regarding the language used in the book, the professor comments, "I don't doubt that many of you may be struggling with the book. Don't be alarmed. I had problems with it as well when I first read it around, oh, three decades ago. Personally, I hated it then and still occasionally have problems with the language used today."

10 Detail Question

Ⓓ The professor points out, "But during the 1800s, the mass education of the time resulted in an increase in the literacy rate, so more and more people began reading.

As a result, much of the writing reflected the common lives of everyday people."

11 Understanding Function Question

Ⓐ When the professor says, "By the way, you should all be reading *Huckleberry Finn*, uh, or be finished with it, by now," she is implying that she assigned the book for the students to read.

PART 1 Lecture #2

p. 143

Script

Listen to part of a lecture in an archaeology class.

M1 Professor: As soon as archaeologists confirm their research and know where they are going to dig, then they're ready to begin the process of excavating a site. When they arrive at the place where they're going to be digging, they must—absolutely must—follow a certain process to ensure that no damage is done to any of the artifacts which are buried underground. First and foremost is the time available for them to dig at a site. If the site is in the countryside or in a place with little human activity and is well protected, the archaeologists can pretty much dig at their own leisure. 🎧17 On the other hand, if the site is in an urban center, then time is of the essence.

M2 Student: In an urban center? **Professor Campbell, that doesn't happen very often, does it?**

M1: I realize it may seem odd, Daniel, but remember that many urban centers are located at vital crossroads or alongside strategic waterways. People have been living in some of these places for thousands of years, so it's only natural that there will be sites of archaeological importance in many cities. In fact, valuable sites are frequently discovered during construction projects in urban areas. When that occurs, developers are almost always forced by the government to halt construction while experts are called in to evaluate the significance of the site. Sometimes the developers pay for the archaeological team to bring in lots of people and the best equipment so that the dig can be done more quickly. After all, the developers want to get back to work constructing their buildings. In these instances, the dig sites are termed rescue excavations by archaeologists because they're trying to examine and preserve as much of the site as they can in a fairly short period of time. That's especially true when the government sets a time limit on how long the archaeologists can dig before construction is permitted to continue.

However, when more time is available, the archaeologists can dig more carefully. The first stage is to dig test holes or trenches. These can give the team an idea as to what's under the layers of ground without having to strip everything away. Of course, uh, if the team has ground-penetrating radar, they can more easily identify places that may hold valuable artifacts. Once the site is examined in one of those two ways, then the top layers of soil are removed. This is often done by excavating machines, which carefully pile the removed soil for further examination. Uh, you know, in case the soil contains any artifacts that may have been overlooked.

The next step involved is the usage of the grid method to organize the site. This superimposes a grid on the entire area so that the site is subdivided into smaller sections for examination. The grid is often in the form of wooden or metal stakes with attached strings or ropes placed in a way to make square sections, each of which is given a name or number. All of the work done and the artifacts found in each section are recorded. That's a practical method which helps archaeologists keep their dig sites organized and lets them become more familiar with the site itself.

After the grid has been set up, it's time to get down to business. So the archaeologists begin digging in sections or places that earlier tests showed may contain items of value. This digging is done carefully with shovels and trowels and, uh, in some cases, even hand brushing. Archaeologists have to carefully remove the soil, which is then carted away in wheelbarrows and is often passed through tiny mesh wire screens to catch any small artifacts that may have been overlooked. If something bigger is found, the dirt is removed with brushes and trowels. This has to be done very carefully to avoid damaging it. In each grid, the soil is dug up in a square shape while the digger carefully makes vertical sides if the soil allows that to happen without collapsing the hole. This enables the person digging to see the stratification of each layer of soil. An important adage in archaeology is that the top layers are from more recent periods while the lower layers are from earlier periods. That's not always the case, but care must be taken not to mix up artifacts from one period with those from another. Archaeologists who are careless and fail to keep artifacts from different periods separate utterly disgrace the entire profession.

While this is going on, there are others recording the work by making drawings, taking photographs, or making video recordings. This is of particular importance when something of significance is found. Once all of the artifacts are discovered and the site is completely excavated, everything needs to be analyzed. Then, the interpretations begin. It may take years to come to various conclusions, and, of course, there will be others who arrive at their own conclusions. Anyway, by following these steps, archaeologists can be sure to excavate a site properly while simultaneously finding and preserving as many artifacts as possible.

Answer Explanations

12 Gist-Content Question

ⓒ The professor mainly discusses which steps archaeologists need to follow when they are excavating sites.

13 Detail Question

ⓐ The professor explains, "Sometimes the developers pay for the archaeological team to bring in lots of people and the best equipment so that the dig can be done more quickly. After all, the developers want to get back to work constructing their buildings. In these instances, the dig sites are termed rescue excavations by archaeologists because they're trying to examine and preserve as much of the site as they can in a fairly short period of time."

14 Detail Question

2, 4 The professor mentions, "The first stage is to dig test holes or trenches. These can give the team an idea as to what's under the layers of ground without having to strip everything away. Of course, uh, if the team has ground-penetrating radar, they can more easily identify places that may hold valuable artifacts."

15 Understanding Attitude Question

ⓑ The professor says, "Archaeologists who are careless and fail to keep artifacts from different periods separate utterly disgrace the entire profession."

16 Understanding Organization Question

ⓓ During the lecture, the professor provides the precise order of the steps that must be taken at a dig site.

17 Understanding Attitude Question

ⓒ When the student asks the question, he implies that he believes there are few dig sites in urban centers.

PART 2 Conversation p. 146

Script

Listen to part of a conversation between a student and a professor.

W Student: Professor Madison, do you have a moment to clear up some questions I have regarding your lecture on the avant-garde movements of the 1800s and 1900s? I'm unsure about a couple of things.

M Professor: Sure, Clarice. I've got a few minutes to spare for you.

W: Thanks so much. Uh, to be blunt, I'm kind of uncertain about the differences between Fauvism and Expressionism.

M: What exactly do you not understand?

W: I understand the parts where you told us about how, when, and where they were established. That was really clear. But, uh, weren't they really the same? I mean, both of them relied upon intense colors for artists to express feelings and emotions in their works. So . . . what's the difference?

M: What you just said is true, but, uh, here . . . Take a look at these two paintings. This one is *The Woman with a Hat* by Henri Matisse. And this one here . . .

W: Oh, I know that one. It's *The Scream* by Edvard Munch.

M: Very good, Clarice. So you tell me . . . How are they different? Oh, and in case you don't know, the Matisse painting is an example of Fauvism while *The Scream* is an Expressionist work.

W: Hmm . . . The colors in *The Woman with a Hat* are very bold. I see lots of green, yellow, and red. But the colors aren't particularly realistic looking.

M: That's correct. That is one thing which really stands out about Fauvist works. The colors are not realistic at all. In fact, they're extremely idealized. Notice how the woman is not painted realistically but is somewhat abstract. Fauvism, while being fairly short lived, was one of the first types of abstract art. People at the time it was being made mostly rejected it, but it gained some measure of respect from critics in later years. Okay, um, so what about *The Scream*? Tell me about it.

W: It's the Expressionist work, right?

M: Correct.

W: Well, you mentioned in class that the Expressionists used violent colors and focused on strong emotions. Uh . . . now that I see the picture, what you said makes perfect sense. It's also a type of abstract art. I mean, uh, you can tell that the person in the painting is human, but his head is almost alien-like in appearance.

M: Well done, Clarice. I knew you could do it. So, uh, as you just described, yes, there are some similarities between the two art movements. After all, they were pretty much contemporary with each other. They were both forms of abstract art, but the end results of their paintings are quite different as you can clearly see.

W: Yes, that's right. I guess I just needed to compare a couple of works to fully understand what you were talking about. I'm not that great at focusing during lectures. I, um, I'm more of a visual learner, so I need to look at paintings to understand the material.

M: In that case, you're attending the right class. Just be sure to listen carefully when I lecture because I'll always mention artists and representative paintings of various movements. If you take the time to check them out after class, you can see the characteristics and features that I discuss in class in the paintings. Just to confirm you understand, let me show you another work by Matisse.

Listen to part of a lecture in a psychology class.

W1 Professor: Most people dream every night. As a general rule, we have no control over what happens in our dreams. They simply occur, and we are like observers in that we can see what happens yet have no ability to influence the events in our dreams. Nevertheless, some people believe they can actually control what happens while their dreaming. This is referred to as lucid dreaming. This phenomenon was first reported by a French researcher in the 1800s and is widely reported nowadays. These days, you can take training sessions on how to engage in lucid dreaming, and there are research institutes and even, uh, Facebook pages dedicated to it.

What you need to know, however, is that while large numbers of people claim to be able to dream lucidly, there remains a great deal of disbelief regarding the entire subject in the psychological community. So I'd like to explore the issue as to whether or not it's possible to control the action in your dreams. Let me first point out that the evidence based on interviewing people just after they wake up from dreaming is hardly concrete. Many people, it appears, believe they can control their dreams . . . But are they correct? Here, uh, I've got some figures for you . . . In 2004, a German study reported that eighty-two percent of people claimed to have had at least one lucid dream in their lives. In 2008, a Japanese study reported that forty-seven percent had made the same claim. In addition, nineteen percent of the people surveyed in Japan claimed to have lucid dreams that occurred as frequently as once a month. A third study, conducted in Brazil, found that seventy-seven percent of those asked claimed to have lucid dreams. Yet another study, uh, conducted in Germany, discovered that people appeared to have more lucid dreams as they got older.

Personally, I'm skeptical of those results. The reason is that they come from surveys asking about people's thoughts and opinions, and the results appear to be way too high. Instead, I'm more impressed with scientific data, which there's actually quite a lot of regarding lucid dreaming.

W2 Student: ∩11Um . . . how can people get scientific data about dreams? I don't get it.

W1: For decades, people have been wired to monitors to examine the science of sleep, and this includes lucid dreaming. What scientists have discovered is that lucid dreaming happens during the REM stage, which is almost at the end of the sleep cycle and is near the time you're about to wake up. Remember that REM stands for rapid eye movement. This stage of sleep got its name because people's eyes appear to flutter rapidly under their eyelids during it.

So we know that dreams occur during REM sleep. But can people deliberately try to dream and then control their dreams? Scientific research seems to indicate that it is possible. Much of this research has been done by British parapsychologist Keith Herne and American psychophysiologist Stephen LaBerge. LaBerge is widely considered the present-day expert on lucid dreaming. Now, uh, in the 1970s, Herne developed a method during which sleepers could indicate that they were dreaming lucidly by shifting their eyes from left to right twice.

M Student: Professor Richardson, I thought the body is paralyzed during REM sleep to prevent people from hurting themselves while dreaming.

W1: That's a good observation, Tom. You're correct in that the body is paralyzed; however, the eyes are not, uh, hence the rapid movement of the eyes during dreaming. Herne's methods were not widely published, and, in the United States, LaBerge independently devised a similar method in the 1980s. LaBerge enhanced the science of lucid dreaming by developing ways to measure the body's responses while engaged in it. Measures of the brain's activity and of the person's breathing and cardiovascular reactions are all taken while an individual is dreaming. LaBerge's observations indicated that a person dreaming lucidly has more brain activity, a higher heart rate, increased respiration, and more sweating than a person dreaming regularly. How did he learn this? Well, after the subjects were awakened and asked if they had been dreaming lucidly, when they said yes, the physical indications almost always matched the ones I just gave you. LaBerge claims that the physical reactions the body undergoes while dreaming lucidly happen as a result of being surprised by being aware of what you're doing and being able to control the events in your own dream.

LaBerge has taken things a step further by developing methods that enable people deliberately to have lucid dreams. He's additionally developed criteria to determine whether or not a person had a lucid dream. Basically, awareness is the key. If someone is aware that he's in a dream, can make decisions, can identify things and people in the dream, can deliberately focus on things and take action, and can then report on all of these things right after waking up, then the person had a lucid dream. So can people control their dreams? I'd say it appears that the answer is yes but that not everyone can do it.

6 Making Inferences Question

(B) The professor tells the students, "What you need to know, however, is that while large numbers of people claim to be able to dream lucidly, there remains a great deal of disbelief regarding the entire subject in the psychological community." So it can be inferred that many experts believe that lucid dreaming is not possible.

7 Understanding Attitude Question

(B) About the surveys, the professor remarks, "Personally, I'm skeptical of those results. The reason is that they come from surveys asking about people's thoughts and opinions, and the results appear to be way too high. Instead, I'm more impressed with scientific data, which there's actually quite a lot of regarding lucid dreaming."

8 Understanding Organization Question

(D) About Herne, the professor states, "Now, uh, in the 1970s, Herne developed a method during which sleepers could indicate that they were dreaming lucidly by shifting their eyes from left to right twice." So she talks about him to cover his method for determining whether someone is dreaming lucidly or not.

9 Detail Question

Fact: 2 , 3   Not a Fact: 1 , 4

About Stephen LaBerge, the professor notes, "LaBerge's observations indicated that a person dreaming lucidly has more brain activity, a higher heart rate, increased respiration, and more sweating than a person dreaming regularly." She also states, "LaBerge claims that the physical reactions the body undergoes while dreaming lucidly happen as a result of being surprised by being aware of what you're doing and being able to control the events in your own dream." She does not, however, mention that LaBerge consulted with Keith Herne or that he wrote a bestselling book.

10 Detail Question

(B) The professor declares, "Basically, awareness is the key. If someone is aware that he's in a dream, can make decisions, can identify things and people in the dream, can deliberately focus on things and take action, and can then report on all of these things right after waking up, then the person had a lucid dream."

11 Understanding Function Question

(C) When the professor makes the comment, she is providing an answer to the question that the student asks about how people can get scientific data about dreams.

Memo